PROSE OF LAKELAND

GRASMERE IN EARLY SPRING

PROSE OF LAKELAND

An Anthology

Compiled by

B. L. THOMPSON

WITH ILLUSTRATIONS BY

W. HEATON COOPER

FREDERICK WARNE & CO. LTD.

LONDON AND NEW YORK

To S. M. T.

Printed in Great Britain

PREFACE

THIS selection of the Prose of Lakeland is intended to be a companion volume to Mrs. Ashley P. Abraham's *Poems of Lakeland*, published in 1934 and reprinted in 1940. An anthology of prose is always more difficult to make than one of poetry, and the present difficulty is the greater because there is such a mass of writing about the Lakes from which to choose. The paragraphs which follow are merely personal pickings, made at intervals over a period of years, and they make no claim to be other than an introduction to our local literature.

To quote sections of Wordsworth's *Guide to the Lakes* and of de Quincey's *Reminiscences of the English Lake Poets*, which are both so full of purple passages, is obviously inevitable, but in order to be more or less representative the book has had to find room not only for the great writers of the Lake District but for the lesser lights as well, for antiquaries, guide-book writers, essayists and topographers. Some of the extracts are long, some short ; some well-known, some almost unknown ; and they come from letters and diaries as well as from " literature " in the ordinary sense of the word. Fiction, a vast field of its own, has been deliberately omitted except that the compiler has allowed himself to quote a passage from Beatrix Potter's *The Fairy Caravan* and Hugh Walpole's brief description of the Lake Country which introduces *The Herries Chronicle*. Dialect has been avoided, as being too difficult to read easily.

The arrangement is, in the main, chronological (though in some cases the original date of publication is uncertain), and this method has the advantage of illustrating the development of the Englishman's attitude to the lakes and mountains, especially in the eighteenth and nineteenth centuries. The original spelling and punctuation of the earlier writings have been preserved, so as to keep their characteristic flavour. Brief introductory notes have been included where necessary, and the sources of all the quotations will be found at the end of the book. The authors' dates, except those of living authors, are given between brackets in the Index.

Grateful thanks are due to the following for leave to reproduce copyright material : The Council of the Cumberland and Westmorland Antiquarian and Archaeological Society for extract 2 ; The Library of the Society of Friends and Messrs. J. M. Dent & Sons Ltd. for the passage from George Fox's Journal ; The Cresset Press Ltd. for part of the Journal of Celia Fiennes ; Messrs. J. M. Dent & Sons Ltd. for the quotation from Defoe's Tour ; The Clarendon Press Ltd. for extract 20, from Professor E. de Selincourt's edition of Wordsworth's Letters ; The Trustees of Dove Cottage, Grasmere, and Messrs. Macmillan & Co. Ltd. for the quotations from Dorothy Wordsworth's Grasmere Journal ; Professor E. Leslie Griggs and the Oxford University Press for extracts 37 and 41, from Hartley Coleridge's Letters ; Messrs. George Allen & Unwin Ltd. for two passages from the Works of John Ruskin ; Messrs. J. M. Dent & Sons Ltd. for three extracts from W. G. Collingwood's *The Lake Counties* ; Messrs. A. & C. Black Ltd. for extract 59 ; Mrs. Rawnsley and Messrs. Jackson, Son & Co. (Booksellers) Ltd. for two descriptive pieces by Canon Rawnsley ; The Executors of Mrs. H. B. Heelis for the passage from *The Fairy Caravan* ; Dr. G. M. Trevelyan, O.M., and The National Trust for part of *Must England's Beauty Perish ?* ; Miss E. M. Ward and Messrs. Methuen & Co. Ltd., for two quotations from *Days in Lakeland ;* The Literary Executors of Sir Hugh Walpole and Messrs. Macmillan & Co. Ltd. for the introductory paragraphs at the beginning of *Rogue Herries* ; the Rev. H. H. Symonds and Messrs. W. & R. Chambers for extract 63 ; and to Mr. W. Heaton Cooper for extracts 68 and 69 and for the delightful illustrations with which he has embellished this small book.

B. L. T.

Troutbeck,
Candlemas, 1954.

CONTENTS

Page

1. WILLIAM CAMDEN : The Keswick Neighbourhood (1586)   13

2. RICHARD BRATHWAITE : The Ferry-boat Accident, Windermere, October 19, 1635 (1636)   15

3. GEORGE FOX : A Crippled Boy at Hawkshead (1653)   17

4. CELIA FIENNES : From Windermere to Ullswater (1698)   18

5. THOMAS ROBINSON : Minerals in the Mountains (1709)   21

6. DANIEL DEFOE : The Borders of Lancashire and Westmorland (1726)   23

7. JOHN BROWN : Derwentwater (1766)   25

8. ARTHUR YOUNG : The Hills Round Keswick (1768)   27

9. THOMAS PENNANT : Windermere (1769)   30

10. THOMAS GRAY : From Keswick to Borrowdale (1769)   33

11. THOMAS GRAY : From Keswick to Kendal (1769)   37

12. WILLIAM GILPIN : The Ullswater Echoes (1772)   40

13. THOMAS WEST : The Tour of the Lakes (1778)   42

14. THOMAS WEST : Crossing the Sands (1778)   44

15. THOMAS WEST : The Stake Pass (1778)   46

16. JAMES CLARKE : Curiosities at Keswick (1787)   48

17. JAMES CLARKE : Herdwick Sheep (1787)   51

18. JOSEPH BUDWORTH : The Ascent of Helm Crag (1792)   52

19. ANN RADCLIFFE : A Ride to the top of Skiddaw (1794)   55

20. WILLIAM WORDSWORTH : With Coleridge to the Lakes (1799)   59

21. S. T. COLERIDGE : Greta Hall, Keswick (1800)   61

22. CHARLES LAMB : Town and Country (1801)   63

23. DOROTHY WORDSWORTH : Grasmere (1801)   65

24. DOROTHY WORDSWORTH : Walks with William and Coleridge (1802)   67

25. S. T. COLERIDGE : A Week's Walking (1802)   69

CONTENTS

		Page
26.	WILLIAM WORDSWORTH: Tarns (1810)	70
27.	WILLIAM WORDSWORTH: Climate (1810)	73
28.	WILLIAM WORDSWORTH: The Colouring of Buildings (1810)	76
29.	JOHN KEATS: Through the Lakes (1818)	80
30.	WILLIAM GREEN: Eagle Crag, Borrowdale (1819)	83
31.	WILLIAM WORDSWORTH: The Rev. Robert Walker of Seathwaite (1820)	85
32.	THOMAS DE QUINCEY: Dove Cottage in Winter (1821)	89
33.	JONATHAN OTLEY: On Meteorology (1823)	93
34.	THOMAS WILKINSON: Haws-water, Kidsty-pike and Mardale (1824)	95
35.	ROBERT SOUTHEY: The Druidical Stones (1829)	97
36.	ROBERT SOUTHEY: Blencathra (1829)	100
37.	HARTLEY COLERIDGE: Grasmere (1830)	104
38.	THOMAS CARLYLE: Sunset amongst Primitive Mountains (1833)	105
39.	J. G. LOCKHART: Sir Walter Scott at the Lakes in 1825 (1837)	107
40.	JOHN RUSKIN: The Mountain Cottage—Westmoreland (1838)	109
41.	HARTLEY COLERIDGE: Greta Hall and Southey (1839)	114
42.	THOMAS DE QUINCEY: Hawkshead in Wordsworth's Schooldays (1839)	115
43.	THOMAS DE QUINCEY: An Excursion over Kirkstone Pass in 1807 (1839)	117
44.	THOMAS DE QUINCEY: Westmoreland Auction Sales (1839)	120
45.	THOMAS DE QUINCEY: The Kendal Highway by Night in 1807 (1839)	122
46.	THOMAS ARNOLD: The Northern Lights from Fox How (1840)	125
47.	JOHN WILSON: Windermere and the Ferry (1842)	126
48.	JOHN WILSON: From Bowness to Troutbeck (1842)	129

CONTENTS

Page

49. HARRIET MARTINEAU : The Ascent of Fairfield (1855)   133

50. CHARLES DICKENS : The Ascent of Carrock (1857)   135

51. EDWIN WAUGH : Cockley Beck (1861)   139

52. E. LYNN LINTON : Up the Duddon (1864)   142

53. R. L. STEVENSON : Down to the Lake at Keswick (1871)   144

54. JOHN RUSKIN : Against the Extension of Railways in the Lake District (1876)   146

55. W. P. HASKETT SMITH : Winter Climbs (1894)   149

56. W. G. COLLINGWOOD : From Ambleside to Grasmere (1902)   151

57. W. G. COLLINGWOOD : Coniston Water, past and present (1902)   152

58. W. G. COLLINGWOOD : Upper Eskdale and the Scafells (1902)   153

59. W. T. PALMER : Small Water (1905)   156

60. H. D. RAWNSLEY : A Sunrise from Helvellyn (1906)   157

61. H. D. RAWNSLEY : Skating on Derwentwater (1913)   160

62. BEATRIX POTTER : Through the Woods to Sawrey (1929)   163

63. G. M. TREVELYAN : Preservation of the Scenery (1929)   165

64. E. M. WARD : Stone Walls (1929)   167

65. E. M. WARD : The Changing Seasons (1929)   170

66. HUGH WALPOLE : The Lake Country (1930)   172

67. H. H. SYMONDS : The High Level Route (1933)   173

68. W. HEATON COOPER : February Snow (1938)   175

69. W. HEATON COOPER : Sunrise on Scafell (1938)   176

SOURCES AND NOTES   178

INDEX TO AUTHORS   183

ILLUSTRATIONS

GRASMERE IN EARLY SPRING   *Frontispiece*

                                              facing page
DERWENTWATER AND SKIDDAW   33
STAKE PASS FROM THE BAND   48
FELL TRACK, EASDALE   69
NAB COTTAGE, RYDAL   76
EAGLE CRAG AND LANGSTRATH   83
SADDLEBACK   94
COTTAGE AT TROUTBECK   115
ULLSWATER FROM GLENCOYNE WOOD   126
RAW HEAD, LANGDALE   145
SKATING ON DERWENTWATER   160
SCAFELL CRAG   165
CONISTON WATER   172

THE KESWICK NEIGHBOURHOOD (1586)

[Camden's " Britannia " was the first great topographical account of this island.]

THE river *Derwent* . . . rising in *Borrodale* (a Vale surrounded with crooked hills) runs among the mountains call'd *Derwent-fells*, wherein at *Newlands* and other places, some rich veins of Copper, not without a mixture of Gold and Silver, were found in our age by *Thomas Thurland* and *Daniel Hotchstetter* a German of Ausburg; tho' discover'd a good while before, as appears from the *Close Rolls* of Henry the third, *n.* 18. About these there was a memorable Trial between our most Serene Queen *Elizabeth*, and *Thomas Percie* Earl of Northumberland and Lord of the Manour; but by virtue of the Royal Prerogative (it appearing that there were also veins of gold and silver) it was carry'd in favour of the Queen. So far is it from being true, what Cicero has said in his Epistles to Atticus, *'Tis well known that there is not so much as a grain of silver in the Island of Britain.* Nor would Caesar, if he had known of these Mines, have told us that the Britains made use of *imported* Copper; when these and some others afford such plenty, that not only all England is supply'd by them, but great quantities exported yearly.

Here is also found abundance of that Mineral-earth or hard shining Stone, which we call *Blacklead*, us'd by Painters in drawing their Lines, and shading such pieces as they do in black and white. Which whether it be *Dioscorides's Pnigitis*, or *Melanteria*, or Ochre, a sort of earth burnt black, is a point I cannot determine, and so shall leave it to the search of others. The *Derwent* falling through these mountains, spreads itself into a spacious Lake, call'd by Bede *Praegrande stagnum*, *i.e.* a vast pool, wherein are three Islands; one, the seat of the famous family of the Ratcliffs, Knights; another inhabited by German Miners; and a third suppos'd

13

to be that wherein Bede tells us *St. Herbert* led a Hermit's life. Upon the side of this, in a fruitful field, encompass't with wet dewy mountains, and protected from the north-winds by that of *Skiddaw*, lyes *Keswick*, a little market-town, formerly a place noted for Mines (as appears by a certain Charter of Edward the fourth) and at present inhabited by Miners. The privilege of a Market was procur'd for it of Edward the first by *Thomas* of *Derwent water*, Lord of the place, from whom it hereditarily descended, to the Ratcliffs.

The *Skiddaw* I mention'd, mounts up almost to the Clouds with its two tops like another Parnassus, and views *Scruffelt*, a mountain of *Anandal* in Scotland, with a sort of emulation. From the Clouds rising up or falling upon these two mountains, the Inhabitants judge of the weather, and have this rhyme common amongst them :

—If Skiddaw hath a cap,
Scruffel wots full well of that.

As also of the height of this and two other mountains in those parts :

Skiddaw, Lauvellin, and Casticand,
Are the highest hills in all England.

THE FERRY-BOAT ACCIDENT, WINDERMERE, OCTOBER 19, 1635 (1636)

FOR the quality of griefe, none knowes it, but hee who hath experimentally and personally felt it. That Place, which hath hitherto beene secured from the least perill, you shall now see personated a spectacle of Sorrow : where those, who vowed in a Sacred and Christian manner, their vowes to Hymen, the Soveraigne of Nuptialls, are now with Tethis to close in wat'ry Funeralls.

The occasion of these sad Obits proceeded from a marriage and a market day, which begot to the Attendants a mournefull night ; yet from that Night (such was their assured expectance, and our undoubted affiance) a happy day. The place, where these drenched Soules were to take Boate, was that famous and renowned Mere of Windermere ; a Mere no less eminent and generously knowne for her Sole-breeding, and peculiar kinde of fishes (commonly called Chares) as for those windy and labyrinthian mazes, with those curiously shaded, beauteously tufted, naturally fortifide, and impregnably seated Ilands in every part of the Mere interveined. To relate the severall windings of it, or more historically to describe it, were fruitles, being already explained by a genuine and learned Relater. To divert then from the Place, to the sad occasion of this Action, thus I proceed.

Windermere, or Winandermere, streaming, or rather staying in a continuate Tract or Channell, without any visible or apparent Current, and dividing the Counties of Westmerland and Lancashire, hath ever constantly kept a Boat for Passengers ; especially those Inhabitants as remaine or reside in the Barrony of Kendall, (a place to her honour, antiently famous for Commerce and industrious Manufacture) as all others, who may have occasion to addresse their course by that passage, to the market of Haukeside, or other places adjoining.

To this Boat, upon a nuptiall but fatall occasion, sundry Passengers, and these all Inhabitants within the Barrony of Kendall, (a Burrough as I formerly observed, highly eminent, by having such neare relation and generall correspondence with most places of trade or trafficke in this Kingdome) repaired ; hoping with a safe and secure gale to arrive, where no perill had ever yet approach'd. The Boat they enter'd, securely confident, with 47 in number, besides other carriages and horses, which (together with the roughnes of the water, and extremity of weather) occasioned this inevitable danger.

Lanch'd had these scarcely to the medth of the water, being scantly a mile broad, but the Boat, either through the pressure and weight which surcharg'd her, or some violent and impetuous windes and waves that surpriz'd her, with all her people, became drench'd in the depths. No succour, no reliefe afforded, for Gods definite Will had so decreed : So as, not one person of all the number was saved : Amongst which, the Bride's Mother, and her Brother in this liquid regiment, equally perished.

A CRIPPLED BOY AT HAWKSHEAD (1653)

AND as I came out of Cumberland, one time, I came to Hawkshead, and lighted at a Friend's house. And there was young Margaret Fell with me and William Caton. And it being a very cold season, we lighted, and the lass made us a fire, her master and dame being gone to the market. And there was a boy lying in the cradle which they rocked, about eleven years old. And he was grown almost double. And I cast my eye upon the boy; and seeing he was dirty, I bid the lass wash his face and his hands, and get him up and bring him unto me. So she brought him to me, and I bid her take him and wash him again, for she had not washed him clean. Then was I moved of the Lord God to lay my hands upon him and speak to him, and so bid the lass take him again and put on his clothes. And after we passed away.

And sometime after I called at the house, and I met his mother, but did not light. "Oh! stay," says she, "and have a meeting at our house, for all the country is convinced by the great miracle that was done by thee upon my son. For we had carried him to Wells and the Bath, and all doctors had given him over, for his grandfather and father feared he would have died and their name have gone out, having but that son; but presently, after you were gone," says she, "we came home and found our son playing in the streets. Therefore," said she, "all the country would come to hear," if I would come back again and have a meeting there. And this was about three years after she told me of it, and he was grown to be a straight, full youth then. So the Lord have the praise.

FROM WINDERMERE TO ULLSWATER (1698)

THENCE I rode almost all the waye in sight of this great water ; some tymes I lost it by reason of the great hills interposeing and so a continu'd up hill and down hill and that pretty steep even when I was in that they called bottoms, which are very rich good grounds, and so I gained by degrees from lower to higher hills which I allwayes went up and down before I came to another hill ; at last I attained to the side of one of these hills or fells of rocks which I passed on the side much about the middle ; for looking down to the bottom it was at least a mile all full of those lesser hills and inclosures, so looking upward I was as farre from the top which was all rocks and something more barren tho' there was some trees and woods growing in the rocks and hanging over all down the brow of some of the hills ; from these great fells there are severall springs out of the rock that trickle down their sides, and as they meete with stones and rocks in the way when something obstructs their passage and so they come with more violence that gives a pleaseing sound and murmuring noise ; these descend by degrees, at last fall into the low grounds and fructifye it which makes the land soe fruit full in the valleys ; and upon those very high fells or rocky hills its (tho') soe high and yet a moorish sort off ground whence they digg abundance of peat which they use for their fewell, being in many places a barren ground yielding noe wood, etc. ; I rode in sight of this Winander Water as I was saying up and down above 7 mile ; afterwards as I was ascending another of those barren fells—which tho' I at last was not halfe way up, yet was an hour going it up and down, on the other side going only on the side of it about the middle of it, but it was of such a height as to shew one a great deale of the Country when it happens to be between those hills, else those interposeing hinders any sight but of the clouds—I see a good way behind me another of those waters or mers

18

but not very bigge; these great hills are so full of loose stones and shelves of rocks that its very unsafe to ride them down.

There is good marble amongst those rocks: as I walked down at this place I was walled on both sides by those inaccessible high rocky barren hills which hang over ones head in some places and appear very terrible; and from them spring many little currents of water from the sides and clefts which trickle down to some lower part where it runs swiftly over the stones and shelves in the way, which makes a pleasant rush and murmuring noise and like a snow ball is encreased by each spring trickling down on either side of those hills, and so descends into the bottoms which are a moorish ground in which in many places the waters stand, and so forme some of those Lakes as it did here, the confluence of all these little springs being gathered together in this Lake which was soe deep as the current of water that passed through it was scarce to be perceived till one came to the farther end, from whence it run a good little river and pretty quick, over which many bridges are laid.

Here I came to villages of sad little hutts made up of drye walls, only stones piled together and the roofs of same slatt; there seemed to be little or noe tunnells for their chimneys and have no morter or plaister within or without; for the most part I tooke them at first sight for a sort of houses or barns to fodder cattle in, not thinking them to be dwelling houses, they being scattering houses here one there another, in some places there may be 20 or 30 together, and the Churches the same; it must needs be very cold dwellings but it shews something of the lazyness of the people; indeed here and there there was a house plaister'd, but there is sad entertainment, that sort of clap bread and butter and cheese and a cup of beer all one can have, they are 8 mile from a market town and their miles are tedious to go both for illness of way and length of the miles.

They reckon it but 8 mile from the place I was at the night before but I was 3 or 4 hours at least going it; here I found a very good smith to shooe the horses, for these stony hills

19

and wayes pulls off a shooe presently and wears them as thinn that it was a constant charge to shooe my horses every 2 or 3 days; but this smith did shooe them so well and so good shooes that they held some of the shooes 6 weeks; the stonyness of the wayes all here about teaches them the art off makeing good shooes and setting them on fast.

Here I cross'd one of the stone bridges that was pretty large which entred me into Cumberlandshire: this river together with the additional springs continually running into it all the way from those vaste precipices comes into a low place and form a broad water which is very cleer and reaches 7 mile in length, Ules water its called, such another water as that of Wiander mer, only that reaches 10 mile in length from Ambleside to the sea, and this is but 7 such miles long; its full of such sort of stones and slatts in the bottom as the other, neer the brimm where its shallowe you see it cleer to the bottom; this is secured on each side by such formidable heights as those rocky fells in same manner as the other was; I rode the whole length of this water by its side sometyme a little higher upon the side of the hill and sometyme just by the shore and for 3 or 4 miles I rode through a fine forest or parke where was deer skipping about and haires, which by means of a good Greyhound I had a little Course, but we being strangers could not so fast pursue it in the grounds full of hillocks and furse and soe she escaped us.

MINERALS IN THE MOUNTAINS (1709)

IN the Mountains of *Newlands*, we meet with several *Veins* of *Mundick Metal*, which consists of *Tin* and *Copper*, so mix'd and incorporated, that their different Species cannot be discerned in the *Ore*, which is of a grey and shining Complexion.

This *Ore* having much *Sulphur* in its Composition, flows easily, and yields near half *Regulus* white, and promising; but the different *Metals* can neither be separated, nor reduced to a malleable Temper.

This seems to be a natural *Bell-Metal*, which is a mixture of *Tin* and *Copper*; and if this *Mundick Metal* were artificially Refin'd and Temper'd, it might in all probability be made as useful, and of equal Value with the artificial Mixture.

In these *Mountains* we have several other *Mundick Veins* of *Copper* and *Iron*, of *Lead* and *Antimony*, mingled in the same *Ore*, but can neither be (by any Art we have) either *separated* or made *malleable*.

The most remarkable *Mundick Vein* upon these *Mountains*, is that we call *Wadd*, or *Black*-Lead.

This *Vein* was found upon *Borrowdale* Mountains, near *Keswick*, and there is not any other of the same kind in *England*, nor perhaps in *Europe*, at least that I ever heard of.

Its Composition is a black, pinguid, and shining Earth, impregnated with *Lead* and *Antimony*. This *Ore* is of more Value than either *Copper*, *Lead*, or *Iron*.

Its natural Uses are both *Medicinal* and *Mechanical*. It's a present *Remedy* for the *Cholick*; it easeth the Pain of *Gravel*, *Stone*, and *Strangury*; and for these and the like Uses, it's much bought up by *Apothecaries* and *Physicians*, who understand more of its *medicinal* Uses, than I am able to give Account of.

The manner of the Country Peoples using it, is thus; First, they beat it small into *Meal*, and then take as much of it in white Wine, or Ale, as will lie upon a *Sixpence*, or more, if the Distemper require it.

It operates by *Urine*, *Sweat*, and *Vomiting*. This Account I had from those who had frequently used it in these Distempers with good Success; besides, those Uses that are *Medicinal*, it hath many other Uses, which increase the Value of it.

At the first discovering of it, the Neighbourhood made no other use of it, but for marking their *Sheep*; but it's now made use of to glazen and harden *Crucibles*, and other Vessels made of *Earth* or *Clay*, that are to endure the hotest *Fire*; and to that end it's wonderfully effectual, which much inhaunceth the Price of such Vessels.

By rubbing it upon *Iron-Arms*, as *Guns*, *Pistols*, and the like, and tingling of them with its Colour, it preserves them from rusting.

It's made use of by Dyers of *Cloath*, making their *Blues* to stand unalterable; for these and other Uses, it's bought up at great Prices by the *Hollanders*, and others.

The *Lords* of this *Vein*, are the Lord *Banks*, and one Mr. *Hudson*. This *Vein* is but opened once in seven Years, but then such quantities of it are got, that are sufficient to serve the Country.

This Mundick *Ore* having little of *Sulphur* in its Composition, will not flow without a violent Heat. It produceth a white *Regulus*, shining like *Silver*. It cannot be made *malleable*.

THE BORDERS OF LANCASHIRE AND WESTMORELAND (1726)

LANCASTER is the next, the county town, and situate near the mouth of the River Lone or Lune. The town is antient; it lies, as it were, in its own ruins, and has little to recommend it but a decayed castle, and a more decayed port (for no ships of any considerable burthen); the bridge is handsome and strong, but, as before, here is little or no trade, and few people. It surprized me to hear that there is not above sixty parishes in all this large county, but many of them are necessarily very large.

This part of the country seemed very strange to us, after coming out of so rich, populous and fruitful a place, as I have just now described; for here we were, as it were, lock'd in between the hills on one side high as the clouds, and prodigiously higher, and the sea on the other, and the sea it self seemed desolate and wild, for it was a sea without ships, here being no sea port or place of trade, especially for merchants; so that, except colliers passing between Ireland and Whitehaven with coals, the people told us they should not see a ship under sail for many weeks together.

Here, among the mountains, our curiosity was frequently moved to enquire what high hill this was, or that; and we soon were saluted with that old verse which I remembered to have seen in Mr. Cambden, viz.

Inglebrough, Pendle-hill and Penigent,
Are the highest hills between Scotland and Trent.

Indeed, they were, in my thoughts, monstrous high; but in a country all mountainous and full of innumerable high hills, it was not easy for a traveller to judge which was highest.

Nor were these hills high and formidable only, but they had a kind of an unhospitable terror in them. Here were

23

no rich pleasant valleys between them, as among the Alps ; no lead mines and veins of rich oar, as in the Peak ; no coal pits, as in the hills about Hallifax, much less gold, as in the Andes, but all barren and wild, of no use or advantage either to man or beast. Indeed here was formerly, as far back as Queen Elizabeth, some copper mines, and they wrought them to good advantage ; but whether the vein of oar fail'd, or what else was the reason, we know not, but they are all given over long since, and this part of the country yields little or nothing at all.

But I must not forget Winander Meer, which makes the utmost northern bounds of this shire, which is famous for the char fish found here and hereabout, and no where else in England ; it is found indeed in some of the rivers or lakes in Swisserland among the Alps, and some say in North Wales ; but I question the last. It is a curious fish, and, as a dainty, is potted, and sent far and near, as presents to the best friends ; but the quantity they take also is not great. Mr. Cambden's continuator calls it very happily the Golden Alpine Trout.

Here we entred Westmoreland, a country eminent only for being the wildest, most barren and frightful of any that I have passed over in England, or even in Wales it self ; the west side, which borders on Cumberland, is indeed bounded by a chain of almost unpassable mountains, which, in the language of the country, are called Fells, and these are called Fourness Fells, from the famous promontory bearing that name, and an abbey built also in antient times, and called Fourness.

DERWENTWATER (1766)

I WOULD sail round the lake, anchor in every bay, and land you on every promontory and island. I would point out the perpetual change of prospects; the woods, rocks, cliffs, and mountains, by turns vanishing or rising into view: now gaining on the sight, hanging over our heads in their full dimensions, beautifully dreadful; and now by a change of situation, assuming new romantic shapes, retiring and lessening on the eye, and insensibly losing themselves in an azure mist.

I would remark the contrast of light and shade, produced by the morning and evening sun; the one gilding the western, and the other the eastern side of this immense amphitheatre; while the vast shadow projected by the mountains, buries the opposite part in a deep and purple gloom, which the eye can hardly penetrate: the natural variety of colouring which the several objects produce, is no less wonderful and pleasing; the ruling tints in the valley being those of azure, green, and gold, yet ever various, arising from an intermixture of the lake, the woods, the grass, and corn-fields; these are finely contrasted by the grey rocks and cliffs; and the whole heightened by the yellow streams of light, the purple hues, and misty azure of the mountains.

Sometimes a serene air and clear sky disclose the tops of the highest hills; at others you see the clouds involving their summits, resting on their sides, or descending to their base, and rolling among the vallies, as in a vast furnace. When the winds are high, they roar among the cliffs and caverns, like a peal of thunder; then too the clouds are seen in vast bodies, sweeping along the hills in gloomy greatness, while the lake joins the tumult and tosses like a sea. But in calm weather, the whole scene becomes new; the lake is a perfect mirror; and the landscape in all its beauty, islands, fields,

25

woods, rocks, and mountains, is seen inverted and floating on its surface.

I will now carry you to the top of a cliff, where if you dare approach the ridge, a new scene of astonishment presents itself, where the valley, lake, and islands seem lying at your feet, where this expanse of water appears diminished to a little pool, amidst the vast immeasurable objects that surround it : for here the summits of more distant hills appear beyond those you had already seen ; and rising behind each other in successive ranges, and azure groups of craggy and broken steeps, form an immense and awful picture, which can only be expressed by the image of a tempestuous sea of mountains.

Let me now conduct you down again, to the valley, and conclude with one circumstance more, which is, that a walk by still moonlight (at which time the distant water-falls are heard in all their variety of sound) among these enchanting dales, opens a scene of such delicate beauty, repose, and solemnity, as exceeds all description.

THE HILLS ROUND KESWICK (1768)

YOUR next view of *Keswick* must be from land, by walking up the vast rocks and crags first described. This is a journey which will terrify those who have been only used to flat countries. The walk to the highest rock is a mile and a half up, and almost perpendicular, horribly rugged, and tremendous ; it is rather a climbing crawl than a walk. The path crossed the stream, which forms the first mentioned cascade, in the midst of dreadful clifts and romantic hollows : The torrent roars beneath you, in some places seen, in others hid by rock and wood.

From hence you climb through a slope of underwood to the edge of a precipice, from which you look down upon the lake and islands in a most beautiful manner ; for coming at once upon them, after leaving a thick dark wood, the emotions of surprize and admiration are very great.

Following the path, (if it may be so called), you pass many romantic spots, and come to a projection of the hill, from which you look down, not only upon the lake as before, but also upon a semi-circular vale of inclosures, of a fine verdure, which gives a curve into the lake : One of the fields is scattered over with trees, which from hence have a picturesque effect.

Advancing further yet, you come to the head of *Crastig-fall*, which is a vast opening among these immense rocky mountains, that lets in between them a view across the lake, catching two of the islands, &c. nor can any thing be more horribly romantic than the adjoining ground where you command this sweet view.

At last we gained the top of the crag, and from it the prospect is truly noble ; you look down upon the lake, spotted with its islands, so far below as to appear in another region ; the lower hills and rocks rise most picturesquely to the view. To the right you look down upon a beautiful vale of cultivated

27

inclosures, whose verdure is painting itself. The town presents its scattered houses, among woods and spreading trees : above it rises *Skiddow*, in the most sublime magnitude.

Descending to the town, we took our leave of this enchanting region of landscape, by scaling the formidable walls of *Skiddow* himself : it is five miles to the top, but the immensity of the view fully repays for the labour of gaining it. You look upon the lake, which here appears no more than a little bason, and its islands but as so many spots ; it is surrounded by a prodigious range of rocks and mountains, wild as the waves, sublimely romantic. These dreadful sweeps, the work of nature in the most violent of her moments, are the most striking objects seen from *Skiddow* ; but in mere extent the view is prodigious. You see the hills in *Scotland* plainly ; you view a fine reach of sea ; command the *Isle of Man*, and see part of an object, which I take to be an highland in *Ireland*; besides prodigious tracks of adjacent country.

Keswick, upon the whole, contains a variety that cannot fail of astonishing the spectator : The lake, the islands, the hanging woods, the waving inclosures, and the cascades are all most superlatively elegant and beautiful ; while the rocks, clifts, crags, and mountains are equally terrifying and sublime. There cannot be a finer contrast. But it is much to be regretted that art does not yield more of her assistance, not in decoration, for the lake wants it not, but in enabling the spectator to command, with greater ease, the luxuriant beauties and striking views, which to so many travellers are hitherto quite unknown : There are many edges of precipices, bold projections of rock, pendent clifts, and wild romantic spots, which command the most delicious scenes, but which cannot be reached without the most perilous difficulty : To such points of view, winding paths should be cut in the rock, and resting places made for the weary traveller : Many of these paths must necessarily lead through the hanging woods, openings might be made to let in views of the lake, where the objects, such as islands, &c. were peculiarly beautiful. At the bottoms of the rocks also, something of the same nature should be executed for the better viewing the cascades, which might be exhibited with a little art, in a variety that would amaze.

It is amusing to think of the pains and expence with which the environs of several seats have been ornamented, to produce pretty scenes, it is true ; but how very far short of the wonders that might here be held up to the eye in all the rich luxuriance of nature's painting. What are the effects of a *Louis's* magnificence to the play of nature in the vale of *Keswick* ! How trifling the labours of art to the mere sport of nature !

It is the contemplation of such amazing scenes, that fills the soul with admiration and almost overpowers her faculties : One is lost in wonder at the omnipotence of a Being, the splendor of whose existence exhibits itself in works of such endless variety.

WINDERMERE (1769)

*[The writer approached the lake at the Ferry Inn on the
Lancashire shore.]*

AFTER breakfast, take boat at a little neighboring creek,
and have a most advantageous view of this beautiful lake,
being favored with a calm day and fine sky. The length of
this water is about twelve miles ; the breadth about a mile ;
for the width is unequal from the multitude of pretty bays,
that give such an elegant sinuosity to its shores, especially
those on the east, or the *Westmoreland* side. The horns of
these little ports project far, and are finely wooded ; as are
all the lesser hills that skirt the water.

At a distance is another series of hills, lofty, rude, grey
and mossy ; and above them soar the immense heights of
the fells of *Conenston*, the mountains of *Wrynose* and *Hardknot*, and the conic points of *Langden* fells ; all except the
first in *Cumberland*.

The waters are discharged out of the South end, at *Newby-
bridge*, with a rapid precipitous current, then assume the name
of *Leven*, and after a course of two miles fall into the estuary
called the *Leven* sands. The depth of this lake is various,
from four yards and a half to seventy-four, and, excepting
near the sides, the bottom is entirely rocky : in some places
are vast subaqueous precipices, the rock falling at once perpendicular, for the depth of twenty-yards, within forty of the
shore ; and the same depth is preserved across the channel.
The fall of the *Leven*, from the lake to high water mark, is
ninety feet ; the deepest part of the lake a hundred and
thirty-two beneath that point.

The boatmen directed their course Northward, and brought
us to the heathy isle of *Lingholm*, and the far projecting cape
of *Rowlinson's Nab*. On the left hand observe the termination
of *Lancashire*, just south of the *Stor*, a great promontory in

30

Westmoreland, all the remaining Western side is claimed by the first ; but Westmoreland bounds the rest, so has the fairest clame to call itself owner of this superb water.

On doubling the *Stor* a new expanse opened before us ; left the little isle of *Crowholme* on the right, traversed the lake towards the horse ferry, and a little beyond, the *great Holme* of thirty acres crosses the water, and conceals the rest. This delicious isle is blessed with a rich pasturage, is adorned with a pretty grove, and has on it a good house.

It has been the fortune of this beautiful retreat often to change masters : the flattering hopes of the charms of retirement have misled several to purchase it from the last cheated owner, who after a little time discovered, that a constant enjoyment of the same objects, delightful as they were, soon satiated. There must be something more than external charms to make a retreat from the world long endurable ; the qualifications requisite fall to the share of a very few ; without them disgust and weariness will soon invade their privacy, notwithstanding they courted it with all the passion and all the romance with which the poet did his mistress.

> Sic ego secretis possum bene vivere sylvis
> Qua nulla humano sit via trita pede.
> Tu mihi curarum requies, tu nocte vel atra
> Lumen, et in solis tu mihi turba locis.

From this island began a new and broader extent of water, bounded on the West by the bold and lofty face of a steep hill, patched with the deep green of vast yews and hollies, that embellished its naked slope. This expanse is varied with several very pretty isles, some bare, others just appear above water, tufted with trees : on the North-East side is the appearance of much cultivation ; a tract near the village of *Boulness* falls gently to the water edge, and rises again far up a high and large mountain, beyond which is a grand skreen of others, the pointed heads of *Troutbeck fells*, the vast rounded mass of *Fairfield*, and the still higher summit of *Rydal*.

Land, and dine in Westmoreland, at *Boulnes*, antiently

called *Winander*, giving name to the lake; and am here treated with most delicate trout and perch, the fish of this water. The charr is found here in great plenty, and of a size superior to those in *Wales*. They spawn about *Michaelmas*, in the river *Brathay*, which, with the *Rowthay* are the great feeds of the lake, preferring the rocky bottom of the former to the gravelly bottom of the other. The fishermen distinguish two varieties, the *case-charr* and the *gelt-charr*, *i.e.* a fish which had not spawned the last season, and esteemed by them the more delicate : this spawns from the beginning of *January* to the end of *March*, and never ascends the river, but selects for that purpose the most gravelly parts of the lake, and that which abounds most with springs. It is taken in greatest plenty from the end of *September* to the end of *November*, but at other times is very rarely met with.

The monks of the abby of *Furness* had a grant from *William* of *Lancaster*, privileging them to fish on this water with one boat and twenty nets ; but in case any of the servants belonging to the abby, and so employed, misbehaved themselves, they were to be chastised by the Lord of the water ; and in case they refused to submit, the abbot was bound to discharge them, and make them forfeit their wages for their delinquency.

Remount my horse, and continue my journey along the sides of the lake, and from an eminence about half a mile N. of the village of *Boulnes*, have a fine view of the water and all it's windings ; and observe that the last bend points very far to the West.

On advancing towards the end have an august prospect of the whole range of these Northern *apennines*, exhibiting all the variety of grandeur in the uniform immense mass, the conic summit, the broken ridge, and the overhanging crag, with the deep chasm-like passages far winding along their bases, rendered more horrible by the blackening shade of the rocks.

DERWENTWATER AND SKIDDAW

FROM KESWICK TO BORROWDALE (1769)

OCTOBER 3. Wind at S.E.; a heavenly day. Rose at 7, and walked out under the conduct of my landlord to *Borrodale*. The grass was covered with a hoar frost, which soon melted, and exhaled in a thin blueish smoke. Crossed the meadows obliquely, catching a diversity of views among the hills over the lake and islands, and changing prospect at every ten paces; left *Cockshut* and *Castlehill* (which we formerly mounted) behind me, and drew near the foot of *Walla-crag*, whose bare and rocky brow, cut perpendicularly down above 400 feet, as I guess, awefully overlooks the way; our path here tends to the left, and the ground gently rising, and covered with a glade of scattering trees and bushes on the very margin of the water, opens both ways the most delicious view, that my eyes ever beheld. Behind you are the magnificent heights of *Walla-crag*; opposite lie the thick hanging woods of Lord Egremont, and *Newland* valley, with green and smiling fields embosomed in the dark cliffs; to the left the jaws of *Borrodale*, with that turbulent chaos of mountain behind mountain, rolled in confusion; beneath you, and stretching far away to the right, the shining purity of the *Lake*, just ruffled by the breeze, enough to shew it is alive, reflecting rocks, woods, fields, and inverted tops of mountains, with the white buildings of *Keswick*, *Crosthwait* church, and *Skiddaw* for a background at a distance. Oh! Doctor! I never wished more for you; and pray think, how the glass played its part in such a spot, which is called Calf-close-reeds; I chuse to set down these barbarous names, that any body may enquire on the place, and easily find the particular station, that I mean. This scene continues to *Barrow-gate*, and a little farther, passing a brook called *Barrow-beck*, we entered *Borrodale*.

The crags, named *Lodoor-banks*, now begin to impend terribly over your way; and more terribly, when you hear, that three years since an immense mass of rock tumbled at once from the brow, and barred all access to the dale (for this is the only road) till they could work their way through it. Luckily no one was passing at the time of this fall; but down the side of the mountain, and far into the lake lie dispersed the huge fragments of this ruin in all shapes and in all directions. Something farther we turned aside into a coppice, ascending a little in front of *Lodoor* water-fall, the height appears to be about 200 feet, the quantity of water not great, though (these three days excepted) it had rained daily in the hills for near two months before : but then the stream was nobly broken, leaping from rock to rock, and foaming with fury. On one side a towering crag, that spired up to equal, if not overtop, the neighbouring cliffs (this lay all in shade and darkness) on the other hand a rounder broader projecting hill shagged with wood and illumined by the sun, which glanced sideways on the upper part of the cataract. The force of the water wearing a deep channel in the ground hurries away to join the lake. We descended again, and passed the stream over a rude bridge. Soon after we came under *Gowder* crag, a hill more formidable to the eye and to the apprehension than that of *Lodoor* ; the rocks a-top, deep-cloven perpendicularly by the rains, hanging loose and nodding forwards, seem just starting from their base in shivers ; the whole way down, and the road on both sides is strewed with piles of the fragments strangely thrown across each other, and of a dreadful bulk. The place reminds one of those passes in the Alps, where the guides tell you to move on with speed, and say nothing, lest the agitation of the air should loosen the snows above, and bring down a mass, that would overwhelm a caravan. I took their counsel here and hastened on in silence.

Non ragionam di lor ; ma guarda, e passa !

The hills here are clothed all up their steep sides with oak, ash, birch, holly, &c. : some of it has been cut 40 years ago, some within these 8 years, yet all is sprung again green, flourishing, and tall for its age, in a place where no soil appears but the staring rock, and where a man could scarce stand upright.

Met a civil young farmer overseeing his reapers (for it is oat-harvest here) who conducted us to a neat white house in the village of Grange, which is built on a rising ground in the midst of a valley. Round it the mountains form an awful amphitheatre, and through it obliquely runs the Derwent clear as glass, and shewing under its bridge every trout that passes. Beside the village rises a round eminence of rock, covered entirely with old trees, and over that more proudly towers Castle-crag, invested also with wood on its sides, and bearing on its naked top some traces of a fort said to be Roman. By the side of this hill, which almost blocks up the way, the valley turns to the left and contracts its dimensions, till there is hardly any road but the rocky bed of the river. The wood of the mountains increases and their summits grow loftier to the eye, and of more fantastic forms: among them appear *Eagle's Cliff, Dove's Nest, Whitedale-pike*, &c. celebrated names in the annals of Keswick. The dale opens about four miles higher till you come to *Sea Whaite* (where lies the way mounting the hills to the right, that leads to the *Wadd-mines*) all farther access is here barred to prying mortals, only there is a little path winding over the Fells, and for some weeks in the year passable to the Dale's-men; but the mountains know well, that these innocent people will not reveal the mysteries of their ancient kingdom, the reign of Chaos and Old Night. Only I learned, that this dreadful road, dividing again leads one branch to *Ravenglas*, and the other to *Hawkshead*.

For me I went no farther than the farmer's (better than 4 m: from Keswick) at *Grange*: his mother and he brought us butter, that Siserah would have jumped at, though not in a lordly dish, bowls of milk, thin oaten cakes, and ale; and we had carried a cold tongue thither with us. Our farmer was himself the man, that last year plundered the eagle's eirie: all the dale are up in arms on such an occasion, for they lose abundance of lambs yearly, not to mention hares, partridge, grouse, &c. He was let down from the cliff in

35

ropes to the shelf of rock, on which the nest was built, the people above shouting and hollowing to fright the old birds, which flew screaming round, but did not dare to attack him. He brought off the eaglet (for there is rarely more than one) and an addle egg. The nest was roundish and more than a yard over, made of twigs twisted together. Seldom a year passes but they take the brood or eggs, and sometimes they shoot one, sometimes the other parent, but the survivor has always found a mate (probably in Ireland), and they breed near the old place. By his description I learn, that this species is the *Erne* (the Vultur *Albicilla* of Linnaeus in his last edition, but in yours *Falco Albicilla*) so consult him and Pennant about it.

Walked leisurely home the way we came, but saw a new landscape : the features indeed were the same in part, but many new ones were disclosed by the midday sun, and the tints were entirely changed. Take notice this was the best or perhaps the only day for going up Skiddaw, but I thought it better employed : it was perfectly serene, and hot as Midsummer.

In the evening walked alone down to the Lake by the side of *Crow-Park* after sun-set and saw the solemn colouring of night draw on, the last gleam of sunshine fading away on the hill-tops, the deep serene of the waters, and the long shadows of the mountains thrown across them, till they nearly touched the hithermost shore. At distance heard the murmur of many water-falls not audible in the day-time. Wished for the Moon, but she was *dark to me, and silent, hid in her vacant interlunar cave*.

FROM KESWICK TO KENDAL (1769)

OCTOBER 8th. Bid farewell to Keswick and took the Ambleside road in a gloomy morning; wind east and afterwards north east; about two miles from the town mounted an eminence called *Castle Rigg*, and the sun breaking out discovered the most beautiful view I have yet seen of the whole valley behind me, the two lakes, the river, the mountain, all in their glory! had almost a mind to have gone back again. The road in some little patches is not completed, but good country road through sound, but narrow and stony lanes, very safe in broad daylight. This is the case about *Causeway-foot*, and among *Naddle-fells* to *Lanthwaite*. The vale you go in has little breadth the mountains are vast and rocky, the fields little and poor, and the inhabitants are now making hay, and see not the sun by two hours in a day so long as at Keswick.

Came to the foot of Helvellyn, along which runs an excellent road, looking down from a little height on Lee's-water, (called also Thirl-meer, or Wiborn-water) and soon descending on its margin. The lake from its depth looks black, (though really as clear as glass) and from the gloom of the vast crags, that scowl over it: it is narrow and about three miles long, resembling a river in its course; little shining torrents hurry down the rocks to join it, with not a bush to overshadow them, or cover their march: all is rock and loose stones up to the very brow, which lies so near your way, that not above half the height of Helvellyn can be seen.

Past by the little chapel of *Wiborn*, out of which the Sunday congregation were then issuing. Past a beck near *Dunmail-raise* and entered Westmoreland a second time, now begin to see *Helm-crag* distinguished from its rugged neighbours not so much by its height, as by the strange broken outline of its top, like some gigantic building demolished, and the stones that composed it flung across each other in wild confusion. Just beyond it opens one of the sweetest landscapes that art ever attempted to imitate. The bosom of the mountains spreading here into a broad bason discovers in the midst *Grasmere-water* ; its margin is hollowed into small bays with bold eminences : some of them rocks, some of soft turf that half conceal and vary the figure of the little lake they command.

From the shore a low promontory pushes itself far into the water, and on it stands a white village with the parish-church rising in the midst of it, hanging enclosures, corn-fields, and meadows green as an emerald, with their trees and hedges, and cattle fill up the whole space from the edge of the water. Just opposite to you is a large farm-house at the bottom of a steep smooth lawn embosomed in old woods, which climb half way up the mountain's side, and discover above them a broken line of crags, that crown the scene. Not a single red tile, no flaming gentleman's house, or garden walls break in upon the repose of this little unsuspected paradise, but all is peace, rusticity, and happy poverty in its neatest, most becoming attire.

The road winds here over *Grasmere-hill*, whose rocks soon conceal the water from your sight, yet it is continued along behind them, and contracting itself to a river communicates with *Ridale-water*, another small lake, but of inferior size and beauty : it seems shallow too, for large patches of reeds appear pretty far within it. Into this vale the road descends : on the opposite banks large and ancient woods mount up the hills, and just to the left of our way stands *Ridale-hall*, the family seat of Sir Mic. Fleming, but now a farm-house, a large old fashioned fabric surrounded with wood, and not much too good for its present destination. Sir Michael is now on his travels, and all this timber far and wide belongs to him, I tremble for it when he returns. Near the house rises a huge crag called *Ridale-head*, which is said to command a full view of *Wynander-mere*, and I doubt it not, for within a mile that great lake is visible even from the road. As to going up the crag, one might as well go up Skiddaw.

Came to *Ambleside* eighteen miles from *Keswick*, meaning

to lie there, but on looking into the best bed-chamber dark and damp as a cellar, grew delicate gave up *Wynander-mere* in despair, and resolved I would go on to *Kendal* directly, fourteen miles farther ; the road in general fine turnpike but some parts (about three miles in all) not made, yet without danger.

Unexpectedly was well rewarded for my determination. The afternoon was fine, and the road for full five miles runs along the side of *Wynander-mere*, with delicious views across it, and almost from one end to the other : it is ten miles in length and at most a mile over, resembling the course of some vast and magnificent river, but no flat marshy grounds, no osier beds, or patches of scrubby plantation on its banks : at the head two valleys open among the mountains, one, that by which we came down, the other Langsledale in which Wrynose and Hard-knot, two great mountains, rise above the rest. From thence the fells visibly sink and soften along its sides, sometimes they run into it, (but with a gentle declivity) in their own dark and natural complexion, oftener they are green and cultivated with farms interspersed and round eminences on the border covered with trees : towards the South it seems to break into larger bays with several islands and a wider extent of cultivation : the way rises continually till at a place called *Orresthead* it turns to South East losing sight of the water.

Passed by *Ing's* chapel and *Stavely*, but I can say no farther for the dusk of the evening coming on I entered *Kendal* almost in the dark, and could distinguish only a shadow of the castle on a hill, and tenter grounds spread far and wide round the town, which I mistook for houses. My inn promised sadly, having two wooden galleries (like Scotland) in front of it. It was indeed an old ill-contrived house, but kept by civil sensible people, so I stayed two nights with them, and fared and slept very comfortably.

THE ULLSWATER ECHOES (1772)

BUT besides the music of winds and tempests, the ecchoes, which are excited in different parts of this lake, are still more grand, and affecting. More or less they accompany all lakes, that are circumscribed by lofty, and rocky screens. We found them on Windermere ; we found them on Derwentwater. But every lake, being surrounded by rocks and mountains of a structure peculiar to itself, forms a variety of instruments ; and, of course, a variety of sounds. The ecchoes therefore of no two lakes are alike ; unless they are mere monotonists.

We took notice of a very grand eccho on the western shores of the great island in Windermere : but the most celebrated ecchoes are said to be found on Ulleswater ; in some of which the sound of a cannon is distinctly reverberated six, or seven times. It first rolls over the head in one vast peal. Then subsiding a few seconds, it rises again in a grand, interrupted burst, perhaps on the right. Another solemn pause ensues. Then the sound arises again on the left. Thus thrown from rock to rock in a sort of aerial perspective, it is caught again perhaps by some nearer promontory ; and returning full on the ear, surprizes you, after you thought all had been over, with as great a peal as at first.

But the grandest effect of this kind is produced by a *successive* discharge of cannon ; at the interval of a few seconds between each discharge. The effect of the first is not over, when the ecchoes of the second, the third, or perhaps of the fourth, begin. Such a variety of awful sounds, mixing, and commixing, and at the same moment heard from all sides, have a wonderful effect on the mind ; as if the very foundations of every rock on the lake were giving way ; and the whole scene, from some strange convulsion, were falling into general ruin.

These sounds, which are all of the terrific kind, are suited

chiefly to scenes of grandeur during some moment of wildness, when the lake is under the agitation of a storm. In a
calm, still evening, the gradations of an eccho, dying away
in distant thunder, are certainly heard with most advantage.
But that is a different idea. You attend then only to the
ecchoes themselves. When you take the *scene* into the combination ; and attend to the effect of the *whole together* ;
no doubt such sounds, as are of the most violent kind, are
best suited to moments of the greatest uproar.

But there is another species of ecchoes, which are as well
adapted to the lake in all it's stillness, and tranquillity, as
the others are to it's wildness, and confusion : and which
recommend themselves chiefly to those feelings, which depend
on the gentler movements of the mind. Instead of cannon,
let a few French-horns, and clarionets be introduced. Softer
music than such loud wind-instruments, would scarce have
power to vibrate. The effect is now wonderfully changed.
The sound of a cannon is heard in bursts. It is the music
only of thunder. But the *continuation* of *musical sounds* forms
a *continuation* of *musical ecchoes* ; which reverberating around
the lake, are exquisitely melodious in their several gradations ;
and form a thousand symphonies, playing together from
every part. The variety of notes is inconceivable. The ear is
not equal to their innumerable combinations. It listens to a
symphony dying away at a distance ; when other melodious
sounds arise close at hand. These have scarce attracted the
attention ; when a different mode of harmony arises from
another quarter. In short, every rock is vocal, and the whole
lake is transformed into a kind of magical scene ; in which
every promontory seems peopled by aerial beings, answering
each other in celestial music.

THE TOUR OF THE LAKES (1778)

SUCH as spend their lives in cities, and their time in crowds, will here meet with objects that will enlarge the mind, by contemplation, and raise it from nature to nature's first cause. Whoever takes a walk into these scenes, must return penetrated with a sense of the Creator's power, in heaping mountains upon mountains, and enthroning rocks upon rocks. Such exhibitions of sublime and beautiful objects cannot but excite at once both rapture and reverence.

When exercise and change of air are recommended for health, the convalescent will find the latter here in the purest state, and the former will be the concomitant of the tour. The many hills and mountains of various heights, separated by narrow vales, through which the air is agitated and hurried on, by a multiplicity of brooks and mountain torrents, keep it in constant circulation, which is known to add much to its purity. The water is also as pure as the air, and on that account recommends itself to the valetudinarian.

As there are few people, in easy circumstances, but may find a motive for visiting this extraordinary region, so more especially those who intend to make the continental tour should begin here; as it will give, in miniature, an idea of what they are to meet with there, in traversing the Alps and Appenines; to which our northern mountains are not inferior in beauty of line, or variety of summit, number of lakes, and transparency of water; not in colouring of rock, or softness of turf; but in height and extent only. The mountains here are all accessible to the summit, and furnish prospects no less surprising, and with more variety than the Alps themselves. The tops of the highest Alps are inaccessible, being covered with everlasting snow, which commencing at regular heights above the cultivated tracts, of wooded and verdant sides, form, indeed, the highest contrast in nature; for there may be seen all the variety of climate in one view. To this, however, we oppose the sight of the ocean, from the summit of all the higher mountains, as it appears intersected with promontories, decorated with islands, and animated with navigation ; which adds greatly to the perfection and variety of all grand views.

Those who have traversed the Alps, visited the lake of Geneva, and viewed Mount Blanc, the highest of the Glaziers, from the valley of Chamouni, in Savoy, may still find entertainment in this domestic tour. To trace the analogy and differences of mountainous countries, furnishes the observant traveller with amusement ; and the travelled visitor of the Cumbrian lakes and mountains, will not be disappointed of pleasure in this particular.

To render the tour more agreeable, the company should be provided with a telescope, for viewing the fronts and summits of inaccessible rocks, and the distant country from the tops of the high mountains Skiddaw and Helvellyn.

The landscape mirror will also furnish much amusement in this tour. Where the objects are great and near, it removes them to a due distance, and shows them in the soft colours of nature, and in the most regular perspective the eye can perceive, or science demonstrate.

The mirror is of the greatest use in sunshine, and the person using it ought always to turn his back on the object that he views. It should be suspended by the upper part of the case, holding it a little to the right or left (as the position of the parts to be viewed require) and the face screened from the sun.

The mirror is a plano-convex glass, and should be the segment of a large circle ; otherwise distant and small objects are not perceived in it ; but if the glass be too flat, the perspective view of great and near objects is less pleasing, as they are represented too near. These inconveniences may be provided against by two glasses of different convexity. The dark glass answers well in sunshine ; but on cloudy and gloomy days the silver foil is better. Whoever uses spectacles upon other occasions, must use them in viewing landscapes in these mirrors.

CROSSING THE SANDS (1778)

FROM Lancaster to Hest-bank, three miles, set out with the Ulverston carriers at the stated hour, or take a guide for the sands that succeed, called Lancaster Sands, and which are 9 miles over. On a fine day there is not a more pleasant sea-side ride in the kingdom. On the right, a bold shore, deeply indented in some places, and opening into bays in others; valleys that stretch far into the country, bounded on each side by hanging grounds, cut into inclosures, interspersed with groves and woods, adorned with sequestered cots, farms, villages, churches, and castles; mountains behind mountains, and others again just seen over them, close the fore scene. Claude has not introduced Socrate on the Tyber in a more happy point of view than Ingleborough appears in during the course of this ride. At entering on the sands, to the left, Heysham-point rises abruptly, and the village hangs on its side in a beautiful manner. Over a vast extent of sands Peel-castle, the ancient bulwark of the bay, rears its venerable head above the tide. In front appears a fine sweep of country sloping to the south. To the right, Warton-cragg presents itself in a bold style. On its arched summit are the vestiges of a square encampment, and the ruins of a beacon. Grounds bearing from the eye, for many a mile, variegated in every pleasing form by woods and rocks, are terminated by cloud-topt Ingleborough.

A little further, on the same hand, another vale opens to the sands and shows a broken ridge of rocks, and beyond them, groups of mountains towering to the sky, Castle-steads, a pyramidal hill, that rises above the station at Kendal, is now in sight. At the bottom of the bay stands Arnside-tower, once a mansion of the Stanleys.

The Cartmel coast, now as you advance, becomes more pleasing. Betwixt that and Silverdale-nab (a mountain of naked grey rock) is a great break in the coast, and through the opening the river Kent rolls its waters to join the tide. In the mouth of the aestuary are two beautiful conical isles, clothed with wood and sweet verdure. As you advance toward them they seem to change their position, and hence often vary their appearance. At the same time a grand view opens of the Westmorland mountains, tumbled about in a most surprising manner. At the head of the aestuary, under a beautiful green hill, Heversham village and church appear in fine perspective. To the north of Whitbarrow scar, a huge arched and bended cliff, of an immense height, shows its stern beaten front. The intermediate space is a mixture of rocks, and woods, and cultivated patches, that form a romantic view.

At the side of the Eau, or river of the sands, a guide on horseback, called *the carter*, is in waiting to conduct passengers over the ford. The prior of Cartmel was charged with this important office, and synodals and peter-pence allowed towards its maintenance. Since the dissolution of the priory, it is held by patent of the duchy of Lancaster, and the salary, twenty pounds per annum, is paid by the receiver-general.

THE STAKE PASS (1778)

WHOEVER chooses an Alpine journey of a very extra-ordinary nature, may return thro' Borrowdale to Amble-side, or Hawkshead. A guide will be necessary from Rosthwaite, over the Stake of Borrowdale (a steep mountain so called) to Langdale Chapel. This ride is the wildest that can be imagined, for the space of eight miles. Above the cultivated tract the dale narrows, but the skirts of the moun-tains are covered with the sweetest verdure, and have once waved with aged wood. Many large roots still remain, with some scattered trees.

Just where the road begins to ascend the Stake, are said to be the remains of a bloomery, close by the water-fall on the left ; but no tradition relates at what time it was last worked. This I could never verify from any visible remains. The mineral was found in the mountain, and the wood used in smelting had covered their steep sides. The masses of iron found on Castle-crag were probably smelted here. Cataracts and water-falls abound on all sides. A succession of water-falls will meet you on the ascent up the Stake, and others will accompany you down the most dreadful descent in Lang-dale. The scenes on the Borrowdale side are in part sylvan and pastoral, on the side of Langdale entirely rocky.

The Stake exhibits a miniature of very bad Alpine road, across a mountain, just not perpendicular, and about five miles over. The road makes many traverses so close, that at every flexture it seems almost to return into itself, and such as are advancing in different traverses, appear to go different ways. In descending the Stake, on the Langdale side, a cataract accompanies you on the left, with all the horrors of a precipice.

Langdale-pike, called Pike-a-stickle, and Steel-pike, is an inaccessible pyramidal rock, and commands the whole. Here nature seems to have discharged all her useless load of matter and rock, when form was first impressed on chaos. Pavey-ark is a hanging rock 600 feet in height, and under it is Stickle-tarn, a large bason of water, formed in the bosom of the rock, and which pours down in a cataract at Mill-beck. Below this, White-gill-crag opens to the centre, a dreadful yawning fissure. Beyond Langdale chapel the vale becomes more pleasing, and the road is good to Ambleside or Hawks-head, by Scalewith-bridge.

CURIOSITIES AT KESWICK (1787)

I AM pleased with an evening walk as well as Dr. Brown or Mr. Gray; yet I had rather be up at four o'clock in a calm morning, and walk about half way up Skiddow, if there is a fog or mist in the valley; for when the mist lyes in the valleys very thick in a morning, the tops of the mountains are quite clear. . . .

About half way up the mountain, or not quite so high, you will be above the mist; which lyes thick and white below. It is quite level, and appears so strong that you might walk upon it; I can compare it to nothing so much as a vast sheet of ice covered with snow; not a house or a tree can be seen; the voice of extremely distant waterfalls is heard perfectly distinct, and not one confusing another.

The loud crowing cock at every cottage, joined to the warbling of the smaller-feathered choir, comes with an almost magical sweetness to the ear, whilst the bellowing bulls and cows form a rural bass to the concert; every sound is much more distinctly heard than at any other time. The words of men conversing at two miles distance are perfectly intelligible; the whistling of the shepherd going to his fleecy care seems close to you, though he cannot be seen. Nor is the eye less delighted, for the tops of distant mountains are now as distinctly viewed with the naked eye, as at other times with the help of a telescope: but these pleasures are of short duration, for as soon as the rising sun gets a little power, the mists quickly disperse, and the objects relapse into their ordinary state.

A person unacquainted with philosophy would wonder what became of these vapours; for very little ever ascends higher than the middle of the mountains, and there seems totally annihilated. I once had two French horns placed in the valley, and another time I heard the hounds running a hare; both of these had a very wonderful and pleasing effect.

STAKE PASS FROM THE BAND

If a traveller should have an opportunity of reviewing this, I would advise him to take a fowling-piece with him, to fire as a signal to his servant (who must remain with another in the valley) that he is above the mist ; then let the servant fire his, and the magnified report will be a matter of great curiosity, and exceed any idea that can be formed.

We now return to the boat, and passing *Barrow-Beck* foot, we enter the chapelry of Borrowdale. We next pass the wooded rocks, *Catt-Gill* and *Catt-Cragg* ; so named I suppose from the wild cats which inhabit there ; and opposite the *Cat-Gill* we see the *Floating Island.*

This Island has its name, from its sometimes being visible for a few days, and then becoming invisible for many weeks, or even months ; at which time it is covered by water to the depth of two fathoms. It is worthy of remark, that the island is never visible unless the water in the lake be high, and then it scarcely appears more than a foot above the surface. This island is about twenty yards in diameter, nearly circular, and slopes gradually from the center to the circumference ; and from thence, as far as the eye can distinguish the sloping is more sudden.

The phaenomena of this island are extremely paradoxical, but may, I think, admit of a very enforced solution. It never appears but when the Lake is swelled with rain, and at that time a very considerable torrent from the adjacent heights comes pouring down *Cat-Gill*, where it sinks among the loose stones : the bottom of the Lake in this part is all covered by a very fine, close grass, with remarkable strong matted roots, seemingly the same kind with the *calomus aromaticus*, and the island lyes but a small distance from the shore. All these circumstances I had an opportunity of observing, not only when I took the soundings, but at many other times ; for I have both stood upon the island and caught fish, and caught them when the boat in which I was lay at anchor over it. Let me now endeavour to solve this paradox : The water which, during a violent rain, pours down the *Cat-Gill*, seems totally lost. It is, however, evident, that it must disembogue itself into the Lake ; I therefore think that this torrent, after running among the loose stones to some distance, endeavours to force its way and mingle with the waters of the Lake ; the toughness of the superincumbent turf prevents this from being easily affected ; the force and weight of the water, therefore, raises the turf into a convex form, and during the continuance of the torrent gives it the appearance of an island. As a farther confirmation of this hypothesis, I once pierced the surface of the island with my fishing-rod ; the grass roots embraced the taper-rod so close, that no water could escape ; but upon withdrawing it, the water spouted to the height of two feet.

HERDWICK SHEEP (1787)

THERE is a kind of sheep in these mountains called *Herdwicks*, which when fed to the highest growth, seldom exceed nine or ten pounds a quarter ; they, contrary to all other sheep I have met with, are seen before a storm, especially of snow, to ascend against the coming blast, and take the stormy side of the mountain, which, fortunately for themselves, saves them from being over-blown.

This valuable instinct was first discovered by the people of *Wasdalehead*, a small village, whose limits join those of Borrowdale. They, to keep this breed as much as possible in their own village, bound themselves in a bond, that no one of them should sell above five ewe (or female) lambs in one year ; means, however, were found to smuggle more, so that all the shepherds now have either the whole or half breed of them ; especially where the mountains are very high, as in *Borrowdale*, *Newlands*, and *Skiddow*, where they have not hay for them in winter. These sheep lye upon the very tops of the mountains in that season as well as in summer ; and, as I said before, keep to the stormy side, where the wind blows the snow off the surface of the ground.

If a calm snow fall, the shepherds take a harrow, and drag it themselves over the tallest heath, or ling ; the snow then falls to the bottom, and the sheep feed upon the tops of it, and the moss which grows upon the stones. They are so remarkably wild and stupid in their temper, that in forcing them by dogs to washing, shearing, &c. they have lain down and died without much fatigue.

Whence this breed first came from I cannot learn ; the inhabitants of *Nether Wasdale* say they were taken from on board a stranded ship, however, till within these few years, their number was very small : they grow very little wool ; eight or nine of them jointly not producing more than a stone, yet their wool is pretty good.

THE ASCENT OF HELM CRAG (1792)

WE went in the morning to Grasmere church; there was a very decent congregation, and the singing was old fashioned and good; and if it had not been for a certain twang at the beginning of every stave, I should have thought them amongst the best country singers I have heard: the men sat on one side of the aisle, the women upon the other, upon rough oak benches, and I could not help observing the *smiles* interchanged when a couple were asked in marriage.

After as good and well-dressed a dinner, at Robert Newton's, as man could wish, we set out to surmount the steep ascent of Helm Crag; but the dinner was so cheap I must mention what it consisted of—Roast pike, stuffed, A boiled fowl, Veal cutlets and ham, Beans and bacon, Cabbage, Pease and potatoes, Anchovey sauce, Parsley and butter, Plain butter, Butter and cheese, Wheat bread and oat cake, Three cups of preserved gooseberries, with a bowl of rich cream in the centre, For two people, at ten pence a head.

We went up a narrow lane that gave us, half a mile from the church, a new view of Grasmere valley, with a perpetual waterfall, justly, from its force, called *White-churn Gill*; it rushes from a crescent-heathed hill, and forms one of the most considerable brooks that supplies Grasmere.

The sun was hot, and after a gentle ascent of about a mile, we rested some minutes under a thick hawthorn, which we will call the foot of the Crag:—the projecting point of the first rise looked formidable, and not less so, to speak in plain English, from having a complete belly full: however, when people are determined to overcome difficulties, time and circumstances are no obstructions.

We were covered from the wind, and it was so steep we were frequently obliged to stop when we met a narrow shelf, and when we got to the first range of the hill I was glad to throw myself down panting for relief:—the grass was slippery,

52

which we guarded against by forcing our sticks as deep into the ground as we possibly could ; and when we had gained the second height, I never remember meeting a more cheerful relief than finding we had got over that part of the hill which kept the wind from us :—this not only enlivened us, but we opened upon prospects which promised to repay our labour when we had surmounted it.

The pinnacle hanging over our right obliged us to take a sweep ; but as we had the wind and a near sight of the top, we found less trouble in this stage than in the others : we were exactly one hour from the hawthorn, which was not from its being a high hill, but the steepest of the country, being seldom frequented but by foxes, sheep, and ravens : our guide was never on it but once, and neither he nor Partridge remember that it has been visited by strangers.

But I must be allowed to rest myself a little before I say any thing of the prospects around us, while I look with awful pleasure at the sight.

We went upon the projecting pinnacle, which had just room to hold two, from which I mark the views, but thought it prudent to have a less exalted rock in order to write them down.

The summit is covered with pieces of rock that give it the features of a grand ruin, occasioned by an earthquake, or a number of stones jumbled together after the mystical manner of the Druids :—there is a deep fissure two feet broad and twenty long, with a stone over one end of it, which gives it the look of a step over a mill stream.

By dropping a small stone down a rent, you hear it rebound a long time ; one bending stone serves as a shelter for sheep, where we found a mushroom, the only one we saw in the north.

The circumference, including its misshapen points, may be above a mile, and where there is any soil the grass is short and sweet : from this unfrequented summit we saw the whole of Windermere. Esthwaite water, and by Grasmere, being our point, they made a complete triangle, divided by rich pastures, &c., whilst the valley and its appendages directly under us seemed to contain every thing that can be beautiful in miniature.

We overlooked the Tarn from whence White-churn Gill has its source, inclosed in a heath horseshoe, whose sides were most brilliantly bespangled with smooth stones, occasioned by a thin sheet of water oozing over them, and an almost perpendicular sun.

We observed over Helvellyn and the Grain of Seat Sandal, a torrent of rain, whilst over Bowness and to the S. East it was collecting so partially the distance gave them the appearance of water spouts : we imagined we had nothing to fear from any of them : it was clear over us ; and in the quarter from whence the wind blew ; the guide had scarcely said so, ere we observed the clouds from Seat Sandal pushing against the wind, though they were considerably exhausted on those mountains : we were soon convinced of our ill judging, and took shelter in the sheep cove, which, by bending, held us secure : this was too confined a situation, and as the rain had somewhat ceased, the guide and I went about one hundred and fifty yards down the hill :—the rain again came on and wet me to the skin, but we were amply repaid by the most luminous sight I ever beheld. I shall attempt to describe it.

The sun shone with such brilliancy through slanting drops, they looked like a line of crystal as round as a finger, and there was a spray intermixed variegated as the rainbow. Newton, who has been all his life accustomed to mountains, says he never saw any thing like it before : might it not be owing to the dark heath over the Tarn, and a partial shining of the sun upon the Crag ?

Too much rain had fallen to render the grass less slippery ; we were obliged to traverse down the hill with the utmost caution, and if not with the difficulty of the ascent with considerably more danger : when we opened Seat Sandal we were surprised by a *superb cataract*, occasioned by the rain which fell whilst we were upon the summit.

I could not help expecting and wishing we should have had a thunder storm.

Let the considerate mind contemplate on the various sights presented to us in so short a space.

A RIDE TO THE TOP OF SKIDDAW (1794)

THE air now became very thin, and the steeps still more difficult of ascent; but it was often delightful to look down into the green hollows of the mountain, among pastoral scenes, that wanted only some mixture of wood to render them enchanting. About a mile from the summit, the way was indeed dreadfully sublime, lying, for nearly half a mile, along the edge of a precipice, that passed with a swift descent, for probably near a mile, into a glen within the heart of Skiddaw; and not a bush nor a hillock interrupted its vast length, or, by offering a midway check in the descent, diminished the fear it inspired.

The ridgy steeps of Saddleback formed the opposite boundary of the glen; and though really at a considerable distance, had, from the height of the two mountains, such an appearance of nearness, that it almost seemed as if we could spring to its side. How much, too, did simplicity increase the sublimity of this scene, in which nothing but mountain, heath, and sky appeared!—But our situation was too critical, or too unusual, to permit the just impressions of such sublimity. The hill rose so closely above the precipice, as scarcely to allow a ledge wide enough for a single horse.

We followed the guide in silence, and, till we regained the more open wild, had no leisure for exclamation. After this, the ascent appeared easy and secure, and we were bold enough to wonder, that the steeps near the beginning of the mountain had excited any anxiety.

At length, passing the skirts of the two points of Skiddaw which are nearest to Derwent water, we approached the third and loftiest, and then perceived that their steep sides, together with the ridges which connect them, were entirely covered near the summits with a whitish shivered slate, which threatens to slide down them with every gust of wind. The broken state of this slate makes the present summits seem like the

55

ruins of others—a circumstance as extraordinary in appearance as difficult to be accounted for.

The ridge on which we passed from the neighbourhood of
the second summit to the third, was narrow, and the eye
reached, on each side, down the whole extent of the mountain
following, on the left, the rocky precipices that impend over
the lake of Bassenthwaite, and looking on the right, into the
glens of Saddleback, far, far below. But the prospects that
burst upon us from every part of the vast horizon, when we had
gained the summit, were such as we had scarcely dared to hope
for, and must now rather venture to enumerate than to describe.

We stood on a pinnacle, commanding the whole dome of
the sky. The prospects below, each of which had been
before considered separately as a great scene, were now miniature parts of the immense landscape. To the north lay, like
a map, the vast tract of low country which extends between
Bassenthwaite and the Irish Channel, marked with the silver
circles of the river Derwent, in its progress from the lake.
Whitehaven, and its white coast, were distinctly seen ; and
Cockermouth seemed almost under the eye. A long blackish
line, more to the west, resembling a faintly-formed cloud,
was said by the Guide to be the Isle of Man, who, however,
had the honesty to confess, that the mountains of Down, in
Ireland, which sometimes have been thought visible, had
never been seen by him in the clearest weather. Bounding
the low country to the north, the wide Solway Firth, with its
indented shores, looked like a grey horizon ; and the double
range of Scottish mountains, seen dimly through the mist
beyond, like lines of dark clouds above it. The Solway
appeared surprisingly near us, though at fifty miles distance ;
and the guide said, that, on a bright day, its shipping could
plainly be discerned.

Nearly in the north, the heights seemed to soften into plains,
for no object was there visible through the obscurity that had
begun to draw over the further distance ; but towards the
east they appeared to swell again ; and what we were told
were the Cheviot hills, dawned feebly beyond Northumberland.
We now spanned the narrowest part of England, looking from

the Irish Channel on one side, to the German Ocean on the other; which latter was however, so far off as to be discernable only like a mist.

Nearer than the County of Durham, stretched the ridge of Cross-fell, and an indistinct multitude of the Westmorland and Yorkshire highlands, whose lines disappeared behind Saddleback, now evidently pre-eminent over Skiddaw, so much so as to exclude many a height beyond it. Passing this mountain in our course to the south, we saw, immediately below, the fells round Derwent-water, the lake itself remaining still concealed in their deep rocky bosom. Southward and westward, the whole prospect was " a turbulent chaos of dark mountains" : all individual dignity was now lost in the immensity of the whole, and every variety of character was overpowered by that of astonishing and gloomy grandeur. Over the fells of Borrowdale, and far to the south, the northern end of Windermere appeared, like a wreath of grey smoke that spreads along a mountain's side. More southward still, and beyond all the fells of the lakes, Lancaster Sands extended to the faintly-seen waters of the sea. Then to the west, Duddon Sands gleamed in a long line among the fells of High Furness. Immediately under the eye, lay Bassenthwaite, surrounded by many ranges of mountains invisible from below. We overlooked all these dark mountains; and saw green cultivated vales over the tops of lofty rocks, and other mountains over these vales, in many ridges : whilst innumerable narrow glens were traced in all their windings, and seen uniting behind the hills with others that also sloped upwards from the lake.

The air on this summit was boisterous, intensely cold, and difficult to be inspired, though below, the day was warm and serene. It was dreadful to look down from nearly the brink of the point on which we stood, upon the lake of Bassenthwaite, and over a sharp and separated ridge of rocks, that from below appeared of tremendous height, but now seemed not to reach half way up Skiddaw; it was almost as if

—the precipitation might down stretch
Below the beam of sight.

Under the lee of an heaped up pile of slates, formed by the customary contribution of one from every visitor, we found an old man sheltered, whom we took to be a shepherd, but afterwards learned was a farmer, and as people in this neighbourhood say, a *statesman*, that is, had land of his own. He was a native, and still an inhabitant of an adjoining vale; but so laborious is the enterprize reckoned, that, though he had passed his life within view of the mountain, this was his first ascent. He descended with us for part of our way, and then wound off towards his own valley, stalking amidst the wild scenery, his large figure wrapped in a dark cloak, and his steps occasionally assisted by a long iron-pronged pike, with which he had pointed out distant objects.

In the descent, it was interesting to observe each mountain below gradually resuming its dignity; the two lakes expanding into spacious surfaces; the many little vallies that sloped upwards from their margins, recovering their variegated tints of cultivation; the cattle again appearing in the meadows; and the woody promontories changing from smooth patches of shade into richly tufted summits. At about a mile from the top, a great difference was perceptible in the climate, which became comparatively warm, and the summer hum of bees was again heard among the purple heath.

We reached Keswick about four o'clock, after five hours passed in this excursion, in which the care of our guide greatly lessened the notion of danger.

WITH COLERIDGE TO THE LAKES (1799)

[This was Coleridge's first visit to the district.]

WE left Cottle, as you know, at Greta Bridge. We were obliged to take the Mail over Stainmore, the road interesting with sun and mist. At Temple Sowerby I learned from the address of a letter lying on the table with the Cambridge post-mark, the letter from Kit to Mrs. C. that he was gone to Cambridge. I learned also from the woman that John was at Newbiggin. I sent a note; he came, looks very well. Your uncle has left you £100, nobody else was named in his will. Having learnt our plans John said he would accompany us a few days.

Next day Thursday we set off, and dined at Mr. Myers; thence to Bampton, where we slept. On Friday proceeded along the lake of Hawes-water (a noble scene which pleased us much). The mists hung so low upon the mountains that we could not go directly over to Ambleside, so went over by Long Sleddale to Kentmere. Next to Troutbeck, and thence by Rayrigg, and Bowness; a rainy and raw day, did not stop at Bowness but went on to the ferry, a cold passage, were much disgusted with the new erections and objects about Windermere; thence to Hawkshead—great change amongst the People since we were last there. Next day Sunday by Rydal and the road by which we approached G. to Robert Newton's, C. enchanted with Grasmere and Rydal.

At Robt. Newton's we have remained till today. John left us on Tuesday; we walked with him to the Tarn. This day was a fine one, and we had some grand mountain scenery; the rest of the week has been bad weather. Yesterday we set off with a view of going to Dungeon Ghyll, the day so bad forced to return. The evening before last we walked to the upper waterfall at Rydal, and saw it through the gloom, and it was very magnificent. C. was much struck with Grasmere and its neighbourhood and I have much to say to you.

You will think my plan a mad one, but I have thought of building a house there by the Lake side. John would give me £40 to buy the ground and for £250 I am sure I could built one as good as we can wish. I speak with tolerable certainty on this head as a Devonshire gentleman has built a cottage there which cost £130 that would exactly suit us every way but the size of the bedrooms ; we shall talk of this. We shall go to Buttermere the day after tomorrow but I think it will be full ten days before we shall see you. There is a small house at Grasmere empty which we might take, but of this we will speak. But I shall write again when I know more on this subject.

GRETA HALL, KESWICK (1800)

[*Coleridge had just come to live at Keswick.*]

My dear Poole,

Your two letters I received exactly four days ago—some days they must have been lying at Ambleside before they were sent to Grasmere, and some days at Grasmere before they moved to Keswick . . . It grieved me that you had felt so much from my silence. Believe me, I have been harassed with business, and shall remain so for the remainder of this year. Our house is a delightful residence, something less than half a mile from the lake of Keswick and something more than a furlong from the town. It commands both that lake and the lake of Bassenthwaite. Skiddaw is behind us ; to the left, the right, and in front mountains of all shapes and sizes. The waterfall of Lodore is distinctly visible.

In garden, etc., we are uncommonly well off, and our landlord, who resides next door in this twofold house, is already much attached to us. He is a quiet, sensible man, with as large a library as yours,—and perhaps rather larger,—well stored with encyclopaedias, dictionaries, and histories, etc., all modern. The gentry of the country, titled and untitled, have all called or are about to call on me, and I shall have free access to the magnificent library of Sir Gilfrid Lawson. I wish you could come here in October after your harvesting, and stand godfather at the christening of my child. In October the country is in all its blaze of beauty.

We are all well and the Wordsworths are well. The two volumes of the " Lyrical Ballads " will appear in about a fortnight or three weeks. Sara sends her best kind love to your mother. How much we rejoice in her health I need not say. Love to Ward, and to Chester, to whom I shall write as soon as I am at leisure. I was standing at the very top of Skiddaw, by a little shed of slate stones on which

I had scribbled with a bit of slate my name among the other names. A lean-expression-faced man came up the hill, stood beside me a little while, then, on running over the names, exclaimed, " Coleridge ! I lay my life that is the *poet Coleridge !* "

God bless you, and for God's sake never doubt that I am attached to you beyond all other men.

S. T. COLERIDGE.

TOWN AND COUNTRY (1801)

[The Wordsworths had invited Lamb to stay with them at Grasmere.]

I OUGHT before this to have replied to your very kind invitation into Cumberland. With you and your sister I could gang anywhere; but I am afraid whether I shall ever be able to afford so desperate a journey. Separate from the pleasure of your company, I don't much care if I never see a mountain in my life. I have passed all my days in London, until I have formed as many and intense local attachments as any of you mountaineers can have done with dead Nature.

The lighted shops of the Strand and Fleet Street; the innumerable trades, tradesmen, and customers, coaches, waggons, playhouses; all the bustle and wickedness round about Covent Garden; the very women of the Town; the watchmen, drunken scenes, rattles; life awake, if you awake, at all hours of the night; the impossibility of being dull in Fleet Street; the crowds, the very dirt and mud, the sun shining upon houses and pavements, the print-shops, the old bookstalls, parsons cheapening books, coffee-houses, steams of soups from kitchens, the pantomimes—London itself a pantomime and a masquerade—all these things work themselves into my mind, and feed me, without a power of satiating me.

The wonder of these sights impels me into night-walks about her crowded streets, and I often shed tears in the motley Strand from fulness of joy at so much life. All these emotions must be strange to you; so are your rural emotions to me. But consider, what must I have been doing all my life, not to have lent great portions of my heart with usury to such scenes?

My attachments are all local, purely local. I have no passion (or have had none since I was in love, and then it was the spurious engendering of poetry and books) for groves and valleys. The rooms where I was born, the furniture which has been before my eyes all my life, a bookcase which has followed me about like a faithful dog, (only exceeding him in knowledge), wherever I have moved, old chairs, old tables, streets, squares, where I have sunned myself, my old school—these are my mistresses.

Have I not enough, without your mountains? I do not envy you. I should pity you, did I not know that the mind will make friends of anything. Your sun, and moon, and skies, and hills, and lakes, affect me no more, or scarcely come to me in more venerable characters, than as a gilded room with tapestry and tapers, where I might live with handsome visible objects.

I consider the clouds above me but as a roof beautifully painted, but unable to satisfy the mind : and at last, like the pictures of the apartment of a connoisseur, unable to afford him any longer a pleasure. So fading upon me, from disuse, have been the beauties of Nature, as they have been confinedly called ; so ever fresh, and green, and warm are all the inventions of men, and assemblies of men in this great city. I should certainly have laughed with dear Joanna.

Give my kindest love, and my sister's, to D. and yourself ; and a kiss from me to little Barbara Lewthwaite. Thank you for liking my play.

GRASMERE (1801)

(*November*) *18th, Wednesday*. We sate in the house in the morning reading Spenser. I was unwell and lay in bed all the afternoon. Wm. and Mary walked to Rydale. Very pleasant moonlight. The Lakes beautiful. The church an image of peace. Wm. wrote some lines upon it in bed when they came home. Mary and I walked as far as Sara's Gate before supper. We stood there a long time, the whole scene impressive, the mountains indistinct, the Lake calm and partly ruffled. Large Island, a sweet sound of water falling into the quiet Lake.

A storm was gathering in Easedale, so we returned ; but the moon came out, and opened to us the church and village. Helm Crag in shade, the larger mountains dappled like a sky. We stood long upon the bridge. Wished for Wm., he had stayed at home being sickish—found him better ; we went to bed.

(*November*) *19th, Thursday*. A beautiful sunny, frosty morning. We did not walk all day. Wm. said he would put it off till the fine moonlight night, and then it came on a heavy rain and wind. Charles and Olivia Lloyd called in the morning.

(*November*) *20th, Friday*. We walked in the morning to Easedale. In the evening we had chearful letters from Coleridge and Sara.

(*November*) *21st, Saturday*. We walked in the morning, and paid one pound and 4d. for letters. William out of spirits. We had a pleasant walk and spent a pleasant evening. There was a furious wind and cold at night. Mr. Simpson drank tea with us, and helped William out with the boat. Wm. and Mary walked to the Swan, homewards, with him. A keen clear frosty night. I went into the orchard while they were out.

(*November*) *22nd, Sunday*. We wrote to Coleridge and

E   65 sent our letter by the boy. Mr. and Miss Simpson came in at tea time. We went with them to the Blacksmith's and returned by Butterlip How—a frost and wind with bright moonshine. The vale looked spacious and very beautiful— the level meadows seemed very large and some nearer us, unequal ground, heaving like sand, the Cottages beautiful and quiet, we passed one near which stood a cropped ash with upright forked branches like the Devil's horns frightening a guilty conscience. We were happy and chearful when we came home—we went early to bed.

WALKS WITH WILLIAM AND COLERIDGE (1802)

April 22nd, Thursday. A fine mild morning—we walked into
Easedale. The sun shone. Coleridge talked of his plan of
sowing the laburnum in the woods. The waters were high,
for there had been a great quantity of rain in the night. I
was tired and sate under the shade of a holly tree that grows
upon a rock, I sate there and looked down the stream. I
then went to the single holly behind that single rock in the
field, and sate upon the grass till they came from the waterfall. I saw them there, and heard Wm. flinging stones into
the river, whose roaring was loud even where I was. When
they returned, William was repeating the poem : " I have
thoughts that are fed by the sun." It had been called to his
mind by the dying away of the stunning of the waterfall when
he came behind a stone.

When we had got into the vale heavy rain came on. We
saw a family of little children sheltering themselves under a
wall before the rain came on ; they sat in a row making a
canopy for each other of their clothes. The servant lass was
planting potatoes near them. Coleridge changed his clothes
—we were all wet. Wilkinson came in while we were at
dinner. Coleridge and I after dinner drank black currants
and water.

April 23rd, 1802, Friday. It being a beautiful morning we
set off at 11 o'clock, intending to stay out of doors all the
morning. We went towards Rydale, and before we got to
Tom Dawson's we determined to go under Nab Scar. Thither
we went. The sun shone and we were lazy. Coleridge
pitched upon several places to sit down upon, but we could
not be all of one mind respecting sun and shade, so we pushed
on to the foot of the Scar. It was very grand when we looked
up, very stony, here and there a budding tree. William
observed that the umbrella yew tree, that breasts the wind,
had lost its character as a tree, and had become something

like to solid wood. Coleridge and I pushed on before. We left William sitting on the stones, feasting with silence ; and C. and I sat down upon a rocky seat—a couch it might be under the bower of William's eglantine, Andrew's Broom. He was below us, and we could see him. He came to us, and repeated poems while we sate beside him upon the ground. He had made himself a seat in the crumbling ground.

After we had lingered long, looking into the vales—Ambleside vale, with the copses, the village under the hill, and the green fields—Rydale, with a lake all alive and glittering, yet but little stirred by breezes, and our own dear Grasmere, first making a little round lake of nature's own, with never a house, never a green field, but the copses and the bare hills enclosing it, and the river flowing out of it. Above rose the Coniston Fells, in their own shape and colour—not man's hills, but all for themselves, the sky and the clouds, and a few wild creatures. C. went to search for something new. We saw him climbing up towards a rock. He called us, and we found him in a bower—the sweetest that was ever seen.

The rock on one side is very high, and all covered with ivy, which hung loosely about, and bore bunches of brown berries. On the other side it was higher than my head. We looked down upon the Ambleside vale, that seemed to wind away from us, the village *lying* under the hill. The fir-tree island was reflected beautifully. We now first saw that the trees are planted in rows. About this bower there is mountain-ash, common-ash, yew-tree, ivy, holly, hawthorn, mosses, and flowers, and a carpet of moss.

Above, at the top of the rock, there is another spot—it is scarce a bower, a little parlour on(ly), not *enclosed* by walls, but shaped out for a resting-place by the rocks, and the ground rising about it. It had a sweet moss carpet. We resolved to go and plant flowers in both these places to-morrow. We wished for Mary and Sara. Dined late. After dinner Wm. and I worked in the garden. C. read letter from Sara.

FELL TRACK, EASDALE

A WEEK'S WALKING (1802)

ON Sunday, August 1st, after morning church, I left Greta Hall, crossed the fields to Portinscale, went through Newlands, where " Great Robinson looks down upon Marden's Bower ", and drank tea at Buttermere, crossed the mountains to Ennerdale, and slept at a farm-house a little below the foot of the lake, spent the greater part of the next day mountaineering, and went in the evening through Egremont to St. Bees, and slept there ; went by the sea-coast as far as Gosforth, then turned off and went up Wasdale, and slept at T. Tyson's at the head of the vale.

Thursday morning crossed the mountains and ascended Scafell, which is more than a hundred yards higher than either Helvellyn or Skiddaw ; spent the whole day among clouds, and one of them a frightening thunder-cloud ; slipped down into Eskdale, and there slept, and spent a good part of the next day ; proceeded that evening to Devock Lake, and slept at Ulpha Kirk ; on Saturday passed through the Dunnerdale Mountains to Broughton Vale, Tarber Vale, and in upon Coniston.

On Sunday I surveyed the lake, etc., of Coniston, and proceeded to Bratha, and slept at Lloyd's house ; this morning walked from Bratha to Grasmere, and from Grasmere to Greta Hall, where I now am, quite sweet and ablute, and have not even now read through your letter, which I will answer by the night's post, and therefore must defer all account of my very interesting tour, saying only that of all earthly things which I have beheld, the view of Scafell and from Scafell (both views from its own summit) is the most heart-exciting.

TARNS (1810)

HAVING spoken of Lakes I must not omit to mention, as a kindred feature of this country, those bodies of still water called TARNS. In the economy of Nature these are useful, as auxiliars to Lakes ; for if the whole quantity of water which falls upon the mountains in time of storm were poured down upon the plains without intervention, in some quarters, of such receptacles, the habitable grounds would be much more subject than they are to inundation. But, as some of the collateral brooks spend their fury, finding a free course toward and also down the channel of the main stream of the vale before those that have to pass through the higher tarns and lakes have filled their several basins, a gradual distribution is effected ; and the waters thus reserved, instead of uniting, to spread ravage and deformity, with those which meet with no such detention, contribute to support, for a length of time, the vigour of many streams without a fresh fall of rain.

Tarns are found in some of the vales, and are numerous upon the mountains. A Tarn, in a *Vale*, implies, for the most part, that the bed of the vale is not happily formed ; that the water of the brooks can neither wholly escape, nor diffuse itself over a large area. Accordingly, in such situations, Tarns are often surrounded by an unsightly tract of boggy ground ; but this is not always the case, and in the cultivated parts of the country, when the shores of the Tarn are determined, it differs only from the Lake in being smaller, and in belonging mostly to a smaller valley, or circular recess. Of this class of miniature lakes, Loughrigg Tarn, near Grasmere, is the most beautiful example. It has a margin of green firm meadows, of rocks, and rocky woods, a few reeds here, a little company of water-lilies there, with beds of gravel or stone beyond ; a tiny stream issuing neither briskly nor sluggishly out of it ; but its feeding rills, from the shortness of their course, so small as to be scarcely visible. Five or six cottages are reflected in its peaceful bosom; rocky and barren steeps rise up above the hanging enclosures; and the solemn pikes of Langdale overlook, from a distance, the low cultivated ridge of land that forms the northern boundary of this small, quiet, and fertile domain.

The *mountain* Tarns can only be recommended to the notice of the inquisitive traveller who has time to spare. They are difficult of access and naked; yet some of them are, in their permanent forms, very grand; and there are accidents of things which would make the meanest of them interesting. At all events, one of these pools is an acceptable sight to the mountain wanderer; not merely as an incident that diversifies the prospect, but as forming in his mind a centre or conspicuous point to which objects, otherwise disconnected or insubordinated, may be referred. Some few have a varied outline, with bold heath-clad promontories; and, as they mostly lie at the foot of a steep precipice, the water, where the sun is not shining upon it, appears black and sullen; and, round the margin, huge stones and masses of rock are scattered; some defying conjecture as to the means by which they came thither; and others obviously fallen from on high—the contribution of ages!

A not unpleasing sadness is induced by this perplexity, and these images of decay; while the prospect of a body of pure water unattended with groves and other cheerful rural images by which fresh water is usually accompanied, and unable to give furtherance to the meagre vegetation around it—excites a sense of some repulsive power strongly put forth, and thus deepens the melancholy natural to such scenes. Nor is the feeling of solitude often more forcibly or more solemnly impressed than by the side of one of these mountain pools: though desolate and forbidding, it seems a distinct place to repair to; yet where the visitants must be rare, and there can be no disturbance.

Water-fowl flock hither; and the lonely Angler may here be seen; but the imagination, not content with this scanty allowance of society, is tempted to attribute a voluntary power to every change which takes place in such a spot, whether it be the breeze that wanders over the surface of the water, or the splendid lights of evening resting upon it in the midst of awful precipices.

> There, sometimes does a leaping fish
> Send through the tarn a lonely cheer;
> The crags repeat the raven's croak
>   In symphony austere:
> Thither the rainbow comes, the cloud,
> And mists that spread the flying shroud,
>   And sunbeams, and the sounding blast.

CLIMATE (1810)

IT may now be proper to say a few words respecting climate, and " skiey influences ", in which this region, as far as the character of its landscapes is affected by them, may, upon the whole, be considered fortunate. The country is, indeed, subject to much bad weather, and it has been ascertained that twice as much rain falls here as in many parts of the island ; but the number of black drizzling days, that blot out the face of things, is by no means *proportionally* great. Nor is a continuance of thick, flagging, damp air so common as in the West of England and Ireland. The rain here comes down heartily, and is frequently succeeded by clear, bright weather, when every brook is vocal, and every torrent sonorous ; brooks and torrents, which are never muddy, even in the heaviest floods, except, after a drought, they happen to be defiled for a short time by waters that have swept along dusty roads, or have broken out into ploughed fields. Days of unsettled weather, with partial showers, are very frequent ; but the showers, darkening, or brightening, as they fly from hill to hill, are not less grateful to the eye than finely interwoven passages of gay and sad music are touching to the ear.

Vapours exhaling from the lakes and meadows after sunrise, in a hot season, or, in moist weather, brooding upon the heights, or descending towards the valleys with inaudible motion, give a visionary character to everything around them ; and are in themselves so beautiful, as to dispose us to enter into the feelings of those simple nations (such as the Laplanders of this day) by whom they are taken for guardian deities of the mountains ; or to sympathize with others who have fancied these delicate apparitions to be the spirits of their departed ancestors. Akin to these are fleecy clouds resting upon the hill-tops ; they are not easily managed in picture, with their accompaniments of blue sky ; but how glorious are they in Nature ! how pregnant with imagination for the poet ! and the height of the Cumbrian mountains is sufficient to exhibit daily and hourly instances of those mysterious attachments.

Such clouds, cleaving to their stations, or lifting up suddenly their glittering heads from behind rocky barriers, or hurrying out of sight with speed of the sharpest edge—will often tempt an inhabitant to congratulate himself on belonging to a country of mists and clouds and storms, and make him think of the blank sky of Egypt, and of the cerulean vacancy of Italy, as an unanimated and even a sad spectacle. The atmosphere, however, as in every country subject to much rain, is frequently unfavourable to landscape, especially when keen winds succeed the rain which are apt to produce coldness, spottiness, and an unmeaning or repulsive detail in the distance ;—a sunless frost, under a canopy of leaden and shapeless clouds, is, as far as it allows things to be seen, equally disagreeable.

It has been said that in human life there are moments worth ages. In a more subdued tone of sympathy may we affirm, that in the climate of England there are, for the lover of Nature, days which are worth whole months,—I might say— even years. One of these favoured days sometimes occurs in spring-time, when that soft air is breathing over the blossoms and new-born verdure, which inspired Buchanan with his beautiful Ode to the first of May ; the air, which, in the luxuriance of his fancy, he likens to that of the golden age— to that which gives motion to the funeral cypresses on the banks of Lethe ;—to the air which is to salute beatified spirits when expiatory fires shall have consumed the earth with all her habitations. But it is in autumn that days of such affecting influence most frequently intervene ;—the atmosphere seems refined, and the sky rendered more crystalline, as the vivifying heat of the year abates ; the lights and shadows are more delicate ; the colouring is richer and more finely harmonized ; and, in this season of stillness, the ear being unoccupied, or only gently excited, the sense of vision becomes more susceptible of its appropriate enjoyments.

A resident in a country like this which we are treating of,

will agree with me, that the presence of a lake is indispensable to exhibit in perfection the beauty of one of these days ; and he must have experienced, while looking on the unruffled waters, that the imagination, by their aid, is carried into recesses of feeling otherwise impenetrable. The reason of this is, that the heavens are not only brought down into the bosom of the earth, but that the earth is mainly looked at, and thought of, through the medium of a purer element.

The happiest time is when the equinoxial gales are departed ; but their fury may probably be called to mind by the sight of a few shattered boughs, whose leaves do not differ in colour from the faded foliage of the stately oaks from which these relics of the storm depend : all else speaks of tranquillity ;— not a breath of air, no restlessness of insects, and not a moving object perceptible—except the clouds gliding in the depths of the lake, or the traveller passing along, an inverted image, whose motion seems governed by the quiet of a time, to which its archetype, the living person, is, perhaps, insensible :—or it may happen, that the figure of one of the larger birds, a raven or a heron, is crossing silently among the reflected clouds, while the voice of the real bird, from the element aloft, gently awakens in the spectator the recollection of appetites and instincts, pursuits and occupations, that deform and agitate the world—yet have no power to prevent Nature from putting on an aspect capable of satisfying the most intense cravings for the tranquil, the lovely, and the perfect, to which man, the noblest of her creatures, is subject.

THE COLOURING OF BUILDINGS (1810)

THE principle that ought to determine the position, apparent size, and architecture of a house, viz. that it should be so constructed, and (if large) so much of it hidden, as to admit of its being gently incorporated into the scenery of Nature—should also determine its colour. Sir Joshua Reynolds used to say, " If you would fix upon the best colour for your house, turn up a stone, or pluck up a handful of grass by the roots, and see what is the colour of the soil where the house is to stand, and let that be your choice."

Of course, this precept given in conversation, could not have been meant to be taken literally. For example, in Low Furness, where the soil, from its strong impregnation with iron, is universally of a deep red, if this rule were strictly followed, the house also must be of a glaring red ; in other places it must be of a sullen black ; which would only be adding annoyance to annoyance. The rule, however, as a general guide, is good ; and, in agricultural districts, where large tracts of soil are laid bare by the plough, particularly if (the face of the country being undulating) they are held up to view, this rule, though not to be implicitly adhered to, should never be lost sight of ;—the colour of the house ought, if possible, to have a cast or shade of the colour of the soil.

The principle is, that the house must harmonize with the surrounding landscape : accordingly, in mountainous countries, with still more confidence may it be said, ' Look at the rocks and those parts of the mountains where the soil is visible, and they will furnish a safe direction.' Nevertheless, it will often happen that the rocks may bear so large a proportion to the rest of the landscape, and may be of such a tone of colour, that the rule may not admit, even here, of being implicitly followed. For instance, the chief defect in the colouring of the Country of the Lakes (which is most strongly felt in the summer season) is an overprevalence of a bluish

76

NAB COTTAGE, RYDAL

tint, which the green of the herbage, the fern, and the woods, does not sufficiently counteract. If a house, therefore, should stand where this defect prevails, I have no hesitation in saying, that the colour of the neighbouring rocks would not be the best that could be chosen. A tint ought to be introduced approaching nearer to those which, in the technical language of painters, are called *warm :* this, if happily selected, would not disturb but would animate the landscape.

How often do we see this exemplified upon a small scale by the native cottages, in cases where the glare of whitewash has been subdued by time and enriched by weather-stains ! No harshness is then seen ; but one of these cottages, thus coloured, will often form a central point to a landscape by which the whole shall be connected, and an influence of pleasure diffused over all the objects that compose the picture. But where the cold blue tint of the rocks is enriched by the iron tinge, the colour cannot be too closely imitated ; and it will be produced of itself by the stones hewn from the adjoining quarry, and by the mortar, which may be tempered with the most gravelly part of the soil. The pure blue gravel, from the bed of the river, is, however, more suitable to the mason's purpose, who will probably insist also that the house must be covered with rough-cast, otherwise it cannot be kept dry ; if this advice be taken, the builder of taste will set about contriving such means as may enable him to come the nearest to the effect aimed at.

The supposed necessity of rough-cast to keep out rain in houses not built of hewn stone or brick, has tended greatly to injure English landscape, and the neighbourhood of these Lakes especially, by furnishing such apt occasion for whitening buildings. That white should be a favourite colour for rural residences is natural for many reasons. The mere aspect of cleanliness and neatness thus given, not only to an individual house, but, where the practice is general, to the whole face of the country, produces moral associations so powerful, that, in many minds, they take place of all others. But what has already been said upon the subject of cottages, must have convinced men of feeling and imagination, that a human dwelling of the humblest class may be rendered more deeply interesting to the affections, and far more pleasing to the eye, by other influences, than a sprightly tone of colour spread over its outside. I do not, however, mean to deny, that a small white building, embowered in trees, may, in some situations, be a delightful and animating object—in no way injurious to the landscape ; but this only where it sparkles from the midst of a thick shade, and in rare and solitary instances ; especially if the country be itself rich and pleasing, and abound with grand forms.

On the sides of bleak and desolate moors, we are indeed thankful for the sight of white cottages and white houses plentifully scattered, where, without these, perhaps everything would be cheerless : this is said, however, with hesitation, and with a wilful sacrifice of some higher enjoyments. But I have certainly seen such buildings glittering at sunrise, and in wandering lights, with no common pleasure. The continental traveller also will remember, that the convents hanging from the rocks of the Rhine, the Rhone, the Danube, or among the Appenines, or the mountains of Spain, are not looked at with less complacency when, as is often the case, they happen to be of a brilliant white. But this is perhaps owing, in no small degree, to the contrast of that lively colour with the gloom of monastic life, and to the general want of rural residences of smiling and attractive appearance, in those countries.

The objections to white, as a colour, in large spots or masses in landscape, especially in a mountainous country, are insurmountable. In Nature, pure white is scarcely ever found but in small objects, such as flowers ; or in those which are transitory, as the clouds, foam of rivers, and snow. Mr. Gilpin, who notices this, has also recorded the just remark of Mr. Locke, of N——, that white destroys the *gradations* of distance ; and, therefore, an object of pure white can scarcely ever be managed with good effect in landscape-painting. Five or six white houses, scattered over a valley, by their obtrusiveness, dot the surface, and divide it into triangles, or other mathematical figures, haunting the eye, and disturbing that repose which might otherwise be perfect. I have seen a single
78

white house materially impair the majesty of a mountain ; cutting away, by a harsh separation, the whole of its base, below the point on which the house stood. Thus was the apparent size of the mountain reduced, not by the interposition of another object in a manner to call forth the imagination, which will give more than the eye loses ; but what had been abstracted in this case was left visible ; and the mountain appeared to take its beginning, or to rise, from the line of the house, instead of its own natural base.

But, if I may express my own individual feeling, it is after sunset, at the coming on of twilight, that white objects are most to be complained of. The solemnity and quietness of Nature at that time are always marred, and often destroyed by them. When the ground is covered with snow, they are of course inoffensive ; and in moonshine they are always pleasing—it is a tone of light with which they accord : and the dimness of the scene is enlivened by an object at once conspicuous and cheerful.

I will conclude this subject with noticing that the cold, slaty colour, which many persons, who have heard the white condemned, have adopted in its stead, must be disapproved of for the reason already given. The flaring yellow runs into the opposite extreme, and is still more censurable. Upon the whole, the safest colour for general use is something between a cream and a dust-colour, commonly called stone colour ;— there are, among the Lakes, examples of this that need not be pointed out.

THROUGH THE LAKES (1818)

My dear Tom,

I cannot make my journal as distinct and actual as I could wish, from having been engaged in writing to George, and therefore I must tell you without circumstance that we proceeded from Ambleside to Rydal, saw the waterfalls there, and called on Wordsworth, who was not at home, nor was any one of his family. I wrote a note and left it on the mantelpiece. Thence on we came to the foot of Helvellyn, where we slept, but could not ascend it for the mist. I must mention that from Rydal we passed Thirlswater, and a fine pass in the Mountains—from Helvellyn we came to Keswick on Derwent Water. The approach to Derwentwater surpassed Windermere—it is richly wooded, and shut in with rich-toned Mountains.

From Helvellyn to Keswick was eight miles to breakfast, after which we took a complete circuit of the Lake, going about ten miles, and seeing on our way the fall of Lowdore. I had an easy climb among the streams, about the fragments of rocks, and should have got I think to the summit, but unfortunately I was damped by slipping one leg into a squashy hole. There is no great body of water, but the accompaniment is delightful ; for it oozes out from a cleft in perpendicular Rocks, all fledged with ash and other beautiful trees. It is a strange thing how they got there. At the south end of the Lake the Mountains of Borrowdale are perhaps as fine as anything we have seen.

On our return from this circuit, we ordered dinner, and set forth about a mile and a half on the Penrith road, to see the Druid temple. We had a fag up hill, rather too near dinnertime, which was rendered void by the gratification of seeing those aged stones on a gentle rise in the midst of the Mountains, which at that time darkened all around, except at the fresh opening of the Vale of St. John. We went to bed rather

fatigued, but not so much as to hinder us getting up this
morning to mount Skiddaw. It promised all along to be fair,
and we had fagged and tugged nearly to the top, when, at half-
past six, there came a Mist upon us, and shut out the view.

We did not, however, lose anything by it : we were high
enough without mist to see the coast of Scotland—the Irish
Sea—the hills beyond Lancaster—and nearly all the large ones
of Cumberland and Westmoreland, particularly Helvellyn and
Scawfell. It grew colder and colder as we ascended, and
we were glad, at about three parts of the way, to taste a little
rum which the Guide brought with him, mixed, mind ye, with
Mountain water. I took two glasses going and one returning.
It is about six miles from where I am writing to the top. So
we have walked ten miles before Breakfast today. We went
up with two others, very good sort of fellows. All felt, on
arising into the cold air, that same elevation which a cold bath
gives one—I felt as if I were going to a Tournament.

Wordsworth's house is situated just on the rise of the foot
of Mount Rydal ; his parlour-window looks directly down
Windermere ; I do not think I told you how fine the Vale of
Grasmere is, and how I discovered " the ancient woman
seated on Helm Crag ". We shall proceed immediately to
Carlisle, intending to enter Scotland on the 1st of July.

July 1st. We are this morning at Carlisle. After Skiddaw,
we walked to Ireby, the oldest market town in Cumberland,
where we were greatly amused by a country dancing-school
holden at the Tun, it was indeed " no new cotillion fresh from
France ". No, they kickit and jumpit with mettle extra-
ordinary, and whiskit, and friskit, and toe'd it and go'd it,
and twirl'd it, and whirl'd it, and stamped it, and sweated it,
tatooing the floor like mad. The difference between our
country dances and these Scottish figures is about the same
as leisurely stirring a cup o' Tea and beating up a batter-
pudding. I was extremely gratified to think that, if I had
pleasures they knew nothing of, they had also some into which
I could not possibly enter. I hope I shall not return without
having got the Highland fling. There was as fine a row of
boys and girls as you ever saw ; some beautiful faces, and

F

one exquisite mouth. I never felt so near the glory of Patriotism, the glory of making by any means a country happier. This is what I like better than scenery. I fear our continued moving from place to place will prevent our becoming learned in village affairs : we are mere creatures of Rivers, Lakes, and Mountains.

Our yesterday's journey was from Ireby to Wigton, and from Wigton to Carlisle. The Cathedral does not appear very fine—the Castle is very ancient, and of brick. The City is very various—old, whitewashed narrow streets—broad red-brick ones more modern—I will tell you anon whether the inside of the cathedral is worth looking at. It is built of sandy red stone or Brick. We have now walked 114 miles, and are merely a little tired in the thighs and a little blistered. We shall ride 38 miles to Dumfries, when we shall linger awhile about Nithsdale and Galloway. I have written two letters to Liverpool. I found a letter from sister George ; very delightful indeed : I shall preserve it in the bottom of my knapsack for you.

EAGLE CRAG AND LANGSTRATH

EAGLE CRAG, BORROWDALE (1819)

SPANNING the Greenup stream, is a wooden bridge, affording, under Eagle Crag, a way to another wooden bridge in Langstrath.

Eagle Crag is a grand towering rock, or collection of perpendicular rocks connected by horizontal spaces of variously coloured vegetation. Its form is fine, and it is a majestic background to many pleasing fore-grounds.

On that part of Eagle Crag which is opposite Greenup, the eagles occasionally built their nests. These birds were so destructive to the lambs, and consequently injurious to the interests of the shepherds, that their extermination became absolutely necessary ; but their building places being inaccessible by footsteps, a dangerous experiment was ventured upon. A man, at the hazard of his life, was lowered by a rope, down the face of the rock, about sixty yards. A piked staff, such as is used by the shepherds when they travel the mountains, was the weapon with which this man defended himself against the attack of the parent bird, while he was robbing their nests of the eggs or eaglets.

If birds, their possession was to be his remuneration ; but if eggs, every neighbouring shepherd gave for each egg five shillings. The nests of these birds were formed of the tender branches of trees, and lined with a sort of grass growing upon the bordering rocks. The number of young taken at one brood is not remembered to have exceeded two ; and when not taken, and capable of flying, they were conducted by the old birds, to a distant country, and not seen afterwards. Of the young lambs on which, during spring, they abundantly feasted, they have often been known to fly away with such as were a month old. In winter they visited the head of the Derwent, where their prey was water-fowl.

An instance is related of an eagle, which, having pounced on a shepherd's dog, carried him to a considerable height ;

but the weight and action of the animal effected his partial liberation, but he left part of his flesh in the eagle's beak. The dog was not killed by the fall,—he recovered of his wound, but was so intimidated, that he would never go that way again. . . .

On the eagles being so frequently robbed of their young, in Greenup, they removed to the opposite side of the crag. At this place, they built two years, but left it for Raven Crag, within the Coom, where, after staying one year only, they returned to their ancient seat, in Eagle Crag; where they built annually during the remainder of their stay in Borrowdale. On the loss of its mate, the remaining eagle left the country, but came back, the following spring, with another. His new consort was, not only of a different species, but considerably smaller than his former companion. This pair built, during fourteen years, in Borrowdale; but, thirty-four years ago, they finally abandoned it for Eskdale. At the last mentioned place they were again disturbed, and the larger bird being afterwards shot, the other fled and returned no more.

THE REV. ROBERT WALKER OF
SEATHWAITE (1820)

IN the year 1709, Robert Walker was born at Under-crag, in Seathwaite ; he was the youngest of twelve children. His eldest brother, who inherited the small family estate, died at Under-crag, aged ninety-four, being twenty-four years older than the subject of this Memoir, who was born of the same mother. Robert was a sickly infant ; and, through his boyhood and youth, continuing to be of delicate frame and tender health, it was deemed best, according to the country phrase, to *breed him a scholar* ; for it was not likely that he would be able to earn a livelihood by bodily labour.

At that period few of these dales were furnished with schoolhouses ; the children being taught to read and write in the chapel ; and in the same consecrated building, where he officiated for so many years both as preacher and schoolmaster, he himself received the rudiments of his education. In his youth he became schoolmaster at Loweswater ; not being called upon, probably, in that situation to teach more than reading, writing, and arithmetic. But, by the assistance of a " Gentleman," in the neighbourhood, he acquired, at leisure hours, a knowledge of the classics, and became qualified for taking holy orders.

Upon his ordination, he had the offer of two curacies : the one, Torver, in the vale of Coniston—the other, Seathwaite, in his native vale. The value of each was the same, *viz.* five pounds *per annum* : but the cure of Seathwaite having a cottage attached to it, as he wished to marry, he chose it in preference. The young person on whom his affections were fixed, though in the condition of a domestic servant, had given promise, by her serious and modest deportment, and by her virtuous dispositions, that she was worthy to become the helpmate of a man entering upon a plan of life such as he had marked out for himself. By her frugality

85

she had stored up a small sum of money, with which they
began housekeeping. In 1735 or 1736, he entered upon his
curacy. . . .

And to begin with his industry : eight hours in each day,
during five days in the week, and half of Saturday, except
when the labours of husbandry were urgent, he was occupied
in teaching. His seat was within the rails of the altar ; the
communion table was his desk ; and, like Shenstone's school-
mistress, the master employed himself at the spinning-wheel,
while the children were repeating their lessons by his side.
Every evening, after school hours, if not more profitably
engaged, he continued the same kind of labour, exchanging,
for the benefit of exercise, the small wheel at which he had
sate, for the large one on which wool is spun, the spinner
stepping to and fro. Thus, was the wheel constantly in
readiness to prevent the waste of a moment's time. Nor was
his industry with the pen, when occasion called for it, less
eager.

Intrusted with extensive management of public and private
affairs, he acted, in his rustic neighbourhood, as scrivener,
writing out petitions, deeds of conveyance, wills, covenants,
&c., with pecuniary gain to himself, and to the great benefit
of his employers. These labours (at all times considerable)
at one period of the year, *viz.* between Christmas and Candlemas, when money transactions are settled in this country,
were often so intense, that he passed great part of the night,
and sometimes whole nights, at his desk. His garden also
was tilled by his own hand ; he had a right of pasturage
upon the mountains for a few sheep and a couple of cows,
which required his attendance ; with this pastoral occupation
he joined the labours of husbandry upon a small scale, renting
two or three acres in addition to his own less than one acre of
glebe ; and the humblest drudgery which the cultivation of
these fields required was performed by himself.

He also assisted his neighbours in haymaking and shearing
their flocks, and in the performance of this latter service he
was eminently dexterous. They, in their turn, complimented
him with the present of a haycock, or a fleece ; less as a

recompense for this particular service than as a general acknowledgment. The Sabbath was in a strict sense kept holy; the Sunday evenings being devoted to reading the Scripture and family prayer. The principal festivals appointed by the Church were also duly observed; but through every other day in the week, through every week in the year he was incessantly occupied in work of hand or mind; not allowing a moment for recreation, except upon a Saturday afternoon, when he indulged himself with a Newspaper, or sometimes with a Magazine.

The frugality and temperance established in his house were as admirable as the industry. Nothing to which the name of luxury could be given was there known; in the latter part of his life, indeed, when tea had been brought into almost general use, it was provided for visitors, and for such of his own family as returned occasionally to his roof, and had been accustomed to this refreshment elsewhere; but neither he nor his wife ever partook of it. The raiment worn by his family was comely and decent, but as simple as their diet; the homespun materials were made up into apparel by their own hands. At the time of the decease of this thrifty pair, their cottage contained a large store of webs of woollen and linen cloth, woven from thread of their own spinning. And it is remarkable that the pew in the chapel in which the family used to sit, remains neatly lined with woollen cloth spun by the pastor's own hands. It is the only pew in the chapel so distinguished; and I know of no other instance of his conformity to the delicate accommodation of modern times.

The fuel of the house, like that of their neighbours, consisted of peat, procured from the mosses by their own labour. The lights by which, in the winter evenings, their work was performed, were of their own manufacture, such as still continue to be used in these cottages; they are made of the pith of rushes dipped in any unctuous substance that the house affords. *White* candles, as tallow candles are here called, were reserved to honour the Christmas festivals, and were perhaps produced upon no other occasions. Once a month, during the proper season, a sheep was drawn from their small mountain flock, and killed for the use of the family; and a cow, towards the close of the year, was salted and dried for winter provision : the hide was tanned to furnish them with shoes.

By these various resources, this venerable clergyman reared a numerous family, not only preserving them, as he affectingly says, " from wanting the necessaries of life ; " but affording them an unstinted education, and the means of raising themselves in society.

In this they were eminently assisted by the effects of their father's example, his precepts, and injunctions : he was aware that truth-speaking, as a moral virtue, is best secured by inculcating attention to accuracy of report even on trivial occasions ; and so rigid were the rules of honesty by which he endeavoured to bring up his family, that if one of them had chanced to find in the lanes or fields anything of the least use or value without being able to ascertain to whom it belonged, he always insisted upon the child's carrying it back to the place from which it had been brought.

DOVE COTTAGE IN WINTER (1821)

AND therefore I will here lay down an analysis of happiness ; and, as the most interesting mode of communicating it, I will give it, not didactically, but wrapped up and involved in a picture of one evening, as I spent every evening during the intercalary year, when laudanum, though taken daily, was to me no more than the elixir of pleasure.

Let there be a cottage, standing in a valley, eighteen miles from any town ; no spacious valley, but about two miles long by three-quarters-of-a-mile in average width—the benefit of which provision is, that all the families resident within its circuit will compose, as it were, one larger household, personally familiar to your eye, and more or less interesting to your affections. Let the mountains be real mountains, between three and four thousand feet high, and the cottage a real cottage, not (as a witty author has it) ' a cottage with a double coach-house '; let it be, in fact (for I must abide by the actual scene), a white cottage, embowered with flowering shrubs, so chosen as to unfold a succession of flowers upon the walls and clustering around the windows, through all the months of spring, summer, and autumn ; beginning, in fact, with May roses, and ending with jasmine.

Let it, however, *not* be spring, nor summer, nor autumn ; but winter, in its sternest shape. This is a most important point in the science of happiness. And I am surprised to see people overlook it, as if it were actually matter of congratulation that winter is going, or, if coming, is not likely to be a severe one. On the contrary, I put up a petition, annually, for as much snow, hail, frost, or storm of one kind or other, as the skies can possibly afford. Surely everybody is aware of the divine pleasures which attend a winter fireside —candles at four o'clock, warm hearth-rugs, tea, a fair tea-maker, shutters closed, curtains flowing in ample draperies on the floor, whilst the wind and rain are raging audibly without,

And at the doors and windows seem to call,
As heaven and earth they would together mell ;
Yet the least entrance find they none at all ;
Whence sweeter grows our rest secure in massy hall.
                              Castle of Indolence.

All these are items in the description of a winter evening
which must surely be familiar to everybody born in a high
latitude.   And it is evident that most of these delicacies cannot
be ripened, without weather stormy or inclement in some way
or other.   I am not "*particular*" whether it be snow, or
black frost, or wind so strong that (as Mr. Anti-slavery
Clarkson says) " you may lean your back against it like a
post ".   I can put up even with rain, provided that it rains
cats and dogs, or, as sailors say, " great guns and marline-
spikes " ; but something of the sort I must have ; and if I
have it not, I think myself in a manner ill-used : for why am
I called on to pay so heavily in winter for coals, candles, etc.,
if I am not to have the article good of its kind ?

No : a Canadian winter for my money, or a Russian one,
where every man is but a co-proprietor with the north wind
in the fee-simple of his own ears.   Indeed, so great an epicure
am I in this matter that I cannot relish a winter night fully,
if it be much past St. Thomas's Day, and have degenerated
into disgusting tendencies towards vernal indications : in fact,
it must be divided by a thick wall of dark nights from all
return of light and sunshine.   Start, therefore, at the first
week of November : thence to the end of January, Christmas
Eve being the meridian line, you may compute the period
when happiness is in season, which in my judgment, enters
the room with the tea-tray.   For tea, though ridiculed by
those who are naturally coarse in their nervous sensibilities,
or are become so from wine-drinking, and are not susceptible
of influence from so refined a stimulant, will always be the
favourite beverage of the intellectual ; and, for my part, I
would have joined Dr. Johnson in a *bellum internecinum*
against Jonas Hanway, or any other impious person who
should have presumed to disparage it.

But here, to save myself the trouble of too much verbal

description, I will introduce a painter, and give him directions for the rest of the picture. Painters do not like white cottages, unless a good deal weather-stained ; but, as the reader now understands that it is a winter night, his services will not be required except for the *inside* of the house.

Paint me, then, a room seventeen feet by twelve, and not more than seven and a half feet high. This, reader, is somewhat ambitiously styled, in my family, the drawing-room ; but, being contrived " a double debt to pay ", it is also, and more justly, termed the library ; for it happens that books are the only article of property in which I am richer than my neighbours. Of these I have about five thousand, collected gradually since my eighteenth year. Therefore, painter, put as many as you can into this room. Make it populous with books ; and, furthermore, paint me a good fire ; and furniture plain and modest, befitting the unpretending cottage of a scholar. And near the fire paint me a tea-table ; and (as it is clear that no creature can come to see one on such a stormy night) place only two cups and saucers on the tea-tray ; and, if you know how to paint such a thing, symbolically or otherwise, paint me an eternal tea-pot—eternal *a parte ante*, and *a parte post* ; for I usually drink tea from eight o'clock at night to four in the morning. And, as it is very unpleasant to make tea, or to pour it out for one's-self, paint me a lovely young woman sitting at the table. Paint her arms like Aurora's, and her smiles like Hebe's ; but no, dear M——! not even in jest let me insinuate that thy power to illuminate my cottage rests upon a tenure so perishable as mere personal beauty ; or that the witchcraft of angelic smiles lies within the empire of any earthly pencil.

Pass, then, my good painter, to something more with its power ; and the next article brought forward should naturally be myself—a picture of the Opium-eater, with his " little golden receptacle of the pernicious drug " lying beside him on the table. As to the opium, I have no objection to see a picture of *that* ; you may paint it, if you choose ; but I apprise you that no " little " receptacle would, even in 1816, answer *my* purpose, who was at a distance from the " stately

Pantheon " and all druggists (mortal or otherwise). No : you may as well paint the real receptacle, which was not of gold, but of glass, and as much like a sublunary wine-decanter as possible. In fact, one day, by a series of happily-conceived experiments, I discovered that it *was* a decanter. Into this you may put a quart of ruby-coloured laudanum ; that, and a book of German metaphysics placed by its side, will sufficiently attest my being in the neighbourhood ; but, as to myself, there I demur.

I admit that, naturally, I ought to occupy the foreground of the picture ; that, being the hero of the piece, or (if you choose) the criminal at the bar, my body should be had into court. This seems reasonable ; but why should I confess on this point to a painter ? or why confess it at all ? If the public (into whose private ear I am confidentially whispering my Confessions, and not into any painter's) should chance to have framed some agreeable picture for itself of the Opium-eater's exterior—should have ascribed to him, romantically, an elegant person or a handsome face—why should I barbarously tear from it so pleasing a delusion ?—pleasing both to the public and to me. No : paint me, if at all, according to your own fancy ; and since a painter's fancy should teem with beautiful creations, I cannot fail, in that way, to be a gainer.

And now, reader, we have run through all the ten categories of my condition, as it stood about 1816–17, up to the middle of which latter year I judge myself to have been a happy man ; and the elements of that happiness I have endeavoured to place before you, in the above sketch of the interior of a scholar's library, in a cottage among the mountains, on a stormy winter evening, rain driving vindictively and with malice aforethought against the windows, and darkness such that you cannot see your own hand when held up against the sky.

ON METEOROLOGY (1823)

BESIDES the permanent beauties of a country diversified by hills and dales, mountains and lakes, there are transient subjects capable of arresting the attention of the contemplative observer ; amongst which are—the mists or fogs—sometimes forming over the surface of the lakes—at other times floating along the sides of the hills—or being collected into clouds, hovering upon the summits of the mountains.

Mountains have been supposed to attract the clouds with which their summits are so frequently enveloped ; but it is more to their agency in forming them, that the accumulation of clouds in mountainous countries may be attributed. Clouds are formed of aqueous particles floating in the atmosphere ; and they serve as an awning, to shield the earth from the violence of the sun's rays in hot weather ; and to protect it from the rigour of a cold winter's night, by obstructing the radiation of heat from its surface. In the clearest weather a portion of water always exists in the atmosphere in the state of an invisible vapour, and the higher the temperature of the air, the greater quantity of vapour it is able to sustain : therefore, when air, fully saturated with vapour, suffers a diminution of its heat, the water is exhibited in the form of mists, clouds, dews, or rain. It has been stated by the late Dr. Hutton of Edinburgh, and more fully exemplified by Mr. Dalton, that the quantity of vapour capable of entering into air, increases in a greater ratio than the temperature ; of course, whenever two volumes of air, of different temperatures, are mixed together, (each being previously saturated with vapour), the mean temperature is not able to support the mean quantity of vapour, and consequently the precipitation of vapour in the form of clouds and rain, is occasioned, not by mere cold, but by a mixture of comparatively cold and warm air. And on this principle, may be explained, most of the phenomena of mist or fog, clouds, dews, and rain. . . .

It has been a matter of surprise to some, that a cloud should seem to remain stationary upon the summit of a high mountain, while the air was moving at a brisk rate. The warm air of a valley being impelled up the inclined plane of a mountain side, into a colder region, is not able to support the same quantity of vapour ; and a cloud is formed in consequence : and although the individual particles of which it is composed, are continually moving forward with the wind ; yet by a perpetual accession of vapour on one side, and dispersion on the other, the cloud may continue to occupy the same place ; although its component parts are successively changed. And in this manner may the materials of a cloud be transported invisibly from the summit of one mountain to that of another.

When a dense cloud settles upon a mountain, the wind frequently blows from it on one side with an increased momentum, while on the opposite side its motion is retarded : and a shower commencing on the hills, is generally preceded in its course by a squall ; the air displaced by the falling rain making its escape along the vallies where it meets with the least resistance.

A covering of snow forms a kind of barrier, between the internal heat of the earth, and that of the atmosphere : being a bad conductor, it preserves the surface of the earth from the severity of cold in winter ; but in spring, excludes it from the genial effects of the solar rays. In the meantime the atmosphere suffers more extensive variations ; the greatest extreme of cold being experienced when the earth is covered with snow. There is no authentic account of snow continuing all the year upon these mountains, but patches are frequently remaining on Scawfell and Helvellyn near the middle of July. And in 1816, a small speck was observed on the former mountain on the 30th of that month.

SADDLEBACK

HAWS-WATER, KIDSTY-PIKE AND MARDALE (1824)

ONE morning, about Midsummer, I took my course through the Vale of Bampton. The lanes were bordered by wild roses, some of them pale as the lily, and others blushed warm in the mountain air. I began to wind among mountains:—clouds of wood on one side contrasted well with the shadow of clouds on the other. As I approached the vicinity of Haws-Water I entered among sheep-farms, and was gratified in seeing the inhabitants of these valleys preparing for or busy with sheep-shearing; which is an occasion of exertion and of merriment, and may be compared to the time of vintage among the southern countries of Europe.

Gathering from the mountains is the employment of the preceding day; when the inhabitants of the higher regions and their offspring hurry down the steeps from their pursuers, the rocks and caverns echoing to the clamour of dogs and the shouts of shepherds. The poor sheep, when parting with its fleece, lies mute as the victim for the slaughter. When released from their bonds, the clamour and confusion of anxious mothers in search of their infant offspring, and the cries of numerous offspring for their lost mothers, are musically plaintive: but as they ascend the mountain, the storm of affection is over in five minutes, the young lambs pacing contentedly by the sides of their parents.

I alighted at Riggindale, surrounded by sheep-folds in abundance; and purposing to ascend Kidsty-Pike, had my horse put into the stable. On discovering what I intended, my kind hostess opposed my going alone: however, alone I set off; but had not gone far up the mountain when I heard a shrill whistle, and, turning round, saw a young female following me at full speed:—it was her daughter who had come after me to be my guide: she had often been a shepherdess on Kidsty-Pike; her father's sheep fed there in

95

summer ; and now her information respecting their pastoral employment, the names of the valleys, the rocks, and the mountains, enlivened our ascent.

In a rock, a few yards from the highest point of the mountain, is a spring. They tell us in the neighbourhood, that a few years ago a thunderbolt struck the rock, and that the spring since has not been so copious. Kidsty-Pike descends in the middle, and at the extremities rises in two peaks, perhaps half a mile asunder. . . .

A gauze in the atmosphere magnified the altitude of mountains : the lowest contents of the valleys could not be seen. I saw nothing to a great distance but a world of dark mountains ; Nanbield, Highstreet, Harterfell, Catchedicam, were pointed out to me by Jane Greenhow. But I am not now contemplating altogether a world of shade : on favoured spots the sun broke forth, and on grey rocks shone with great beauty. These rocks were fringed with green, and it altogether seemed a dark ground set with brilliants.

Descending from Kidsty-Pike, my attention is directed to the valleys. Lake and mountain-scenery is unvarying in the progress of time, save occasionally in the introduction of wood, and the beautiful accompaniments of cottages and farmhouses. In the valleys through which I am now advancing, the cottages, sheltered by a few sycamores, are built from and assimilate well with the grey rocks of the mountains ; and their rustic architecture has not changed for ages. This suggests contentment in the inhabitants ; and contentment is a pleasing idea to entertain of one's fellow-creatures.

35: ROBERT SOUTHEY

THE DRUIDICAL STONES (1829)

INCLINATION would lead me to hibernate during half the year in this uncomfortable climate of Great Britain, where few men who have tasted the enjoyments of a better would willingly take up their abode, if it were not for the habits, and still more for the ties and duties which root us to our native soil. I envy the Turks for their sedentary constitutions, which seem no more to require exercise than an oyster does, or a toad in a stone. In this respect, I am by disposition as true a Turk as the Grand Seignior himself ; and approach much nearer to one in the habit of inaction, than any person of my acquaintance. Willing however as I should be to believe, that any thing which is habitually necessary for a sound body, would be unerringly indicated by an habitual disposition for it, and that if exercise were as needful as food for the preservation of the animal economy, the desire of motion would recur not less regularly than hunger and thirst, it is a theory which will not bear the test ; and this I know by experience.

On a grey sober day, therefore, and in a tone of mind quite accordant with the season, I went out unwillingly to take the air, though if taking physic would have answered the same purpose, the dose would have been preferred as the shortest, and for that reason the least unpleasant remedy. Even on such occasions as this, it is desirable to propose to oneself some object for the satisfaction of accomplishing it, and to set out with the intention of reaching some fixed point, though it should be nothing better than a mile-stone, or a directing post. So I walked to the Circle of Stones upon the Penrith road, because there is a long hill upon the way which would give the muscles some work to perform ; and because the sight of this rude monument which has stood during so many centuries, and is likely, if left to itself, to outlast any edifice that man could have erected, gives me always a feeling, which, however often it may be repeated, loses nothing of its force.

The circle is of the rudest kind, consisting of single stones, unhewn, and chosen without any regard to shape or magnitude, being of all sizes, from seven or eight feet in height, to three or four. The circle however is complete, and is thirty-three paces in diameter. Concerning this, like all similar monuments in Great Britain, the popular superstition prevails, that no two persons can number the stones alike, and that no person will ever find a second counting confirm the first. My children have often disappointed their natural inclination to believe this wonder, by putting it to the test and disproving it. The number of the stones which compose the circle, is thirty-eight, and besides these, there are ten which form three sides of a little square within, on the eastern side, three stones of the circle itself forming the fourth ; this being evidently the place where the Druids who presided had their station ; or where the more sacred and important part of the rites and ceremonies (whatever they may have been) were performed. All this is as perfect at this day, as when the Cambrian Bards, according to the custom of their ancient order, described by my old acquaintances, the living members of the Chair of Glamorgan, met there for the last time

> On the green turf and under the blue sky,
> Their heads in reverence bare, and bare of foot.

The site also precisely accords with the description which Edward Williams and William Owen give of the situation required for such meeting places :—

> . . . a high hill top,
> Nor bowered with trees, nor broken by the plough:
> Remote from human dwellings and the stir
> Of human life, and open to the breath
> And to the eye of Heaven.

The high hill is now inclosed and cultivated ; and a clump of larches has been planted within the circle, for the purpose of protecting an oak in the centre, the owner of the field having wished to rear one there with a commendable feeling, because that tree was held sacred by the Druids, and therefore, he supposed, might be appropriately placed there. The whole plantation however has been so miserably storm-stricken, that the poor stunted trees are not even worth the trouble of cutting them down for fuel, and so they continue to disfigure the spot. In all other respects this impressive monument of former times is carefully preserved; the soil within the inclosure is not broken, a path from the road is left, and in latter times a stepping-stile has been placed to accommodate Lakers with an easier access, than by striding over the gate beside it.

The spot itself is the most commanding which could be chosen in this part of the country, without climbing a mountain. Derwent-water and the Vale of Keswick are not seen from it, only the mountains which inclose them on the south and west. Lattrigg and the huge side of Skiddaw are on the north; to the east is the open country toward Penrith, expanding from the Vale of St. John's, and extending for many miles, with Mell-fell in the distance, where it rises alone like a huge tumulus on the right, and Blencathra on the left, rent into deep ravines. On the south-east is the range of Helvellin, from its termination at Wanthwaite Crags to its loftiest summits, and to Dunmailrais. The lower range of Nathdale-fells lies nearer in a parallel line with Helvellin; and the dale itself, with its little streamlet immediately below. The heights above Leatheswater, with the Borrowdale mountains, complete the panorama.

BLENCATHRA (1829)

OF the very many Tourists who are annually brought to
this Land of Lakes by what have now become the migra-
tory habits of the opulent classes, there is a great proportion
of persons who are desirous of making the shortest possible
tarriance in any place ; whose object is to get through their
undertaking with as little trouble as they can, and whose
inquiries are mainly directed to find out what it is not necessary for them to see ; happy when they are comforted with
the assurance, that it is by no means required of them to
deviate from the regular track, and that that which cannot
be seen easily, need not be taken at all. In this way our
hoi polloi take their degree as Lakers.

Nevertheless, the number of those who truly enjoy the
opportunities which are thus afforded them, and have a
genuine generous delight in beholding the grandeur and the
lovelier scenes of a mountainous region, is sufficient to render
this a good and wholesome fashion. The pleasure which
they partake conduces as much to moral and intellectual
improvement, as to health, and present hilarity. It produces
no distaste for other scenes, no satiety, nor other exhaustion
than what brings with it its own remedy in sound sleep. Instead of these, increase of appetite grows here by what it
feeds on, and they learn to seek and find pleasure of the
same kind in tamer landscapes. They who have acquired
in these countries a love of natural scenery, carry with them
in that love a perpetual source of enjoyment ; resembling
in this respect the artist, who, in whatever scenes he may be
placed, is never at a loss for something from which his pencil
may draw forth a beauty, which uncultivated eyes would fail
to discover in the object itself.

In every country, however poor, . . . there is something
of " free Nature's grace " ; . . . where-ever there is wood and
water, wherever there are green fields, . . . wherever there

is an open sky, the feeling which has been called forth, or fostered among the mountains, may be sustained. It is one of our most abiding as well as of our purest enjoyments, . . . a sentiment which seems at once to humble and exalt us, which from natural emotion leads us to devotional thoughts and religious aspirations, grows therefore with our growth, and strengthens when our strength is failing us.

I wonder not at those heathens who worshipped in high places. There is an elasticity in the mountain air, which causes an excitement of spirits, in its immediate effect like that of wine when, taken in due measure, it gladdens the heart of man. The height and the extent of the surrounding objects seem to produce a correspondent expansion and elevation of mind; and the silence and solitude contributes to this emotion. You feel as if in another region, almost in another world. If a tourist in this country inquires which of our mountains it may be worth his while to ascend, he may be told any, or all. Helvellyn and Skiddaw and Blencathra, Scawfell and Great Gable, Hindsgarth and Causey Pike, each is unlike all the others in the prospect that it presents, each has features of its own, and all may well repay the labour of ascending them.

They who would ascend this mountain, should go from Keswick about six miles along the Penrith road, then take the road which branches from it on the left, (proceeding along the mountain side toward Heskett Newmarket), and begin to ascend a little way farther on by a green shepherd's path, distinctly marked, on the left side of a gill. That path may be followed on the mountain toward a little stream which issues from Threlkeld Tarn; you leave it, keeping the stream on the right, and mount a short and rugged ascent, up which a horse may be led without difficulty; and thus, with little fatigue, the Tarn is reached. A wild spot it is as ever was chosen by a cheerful party where to rest, and take their merry repast upon a summer's day. The green mountain, the dark pool, the crag under which it lies, and the little stream which steals from it, are the only objects; the gentle voice of that stream the only sound, unless a kite be wheeling above, or a sheep bleats on the fell side. A silent, solitary place ; and such solitude heightens social enjoyment, as much as it conduces to lonely meditation.

Ascending from hence toward the brow of the mountain, you look back through the opening, where the stream finds its way, to a distant view of the open country about Penrith, with the long line of Crossfell bounding it. When the brow is reached, you are on the edge of that bold and rugged front which Blencathra presents when seen from the road to Matterdale, or from the Vale of St. John's. A portion of the hill, (Hallfell it is called), somewhat pyramidical in shape, stands out here like an enormous buttress, separated from the body of the mountain on all sides by deep ravines. These have apparently been formed by some water-spout, bursting upon what was once the green breast of the mountain, and thus opening water-courses, which the rain and storms have continually been deepening.

In looking down these ravines from the brow you have a sense of perfect security ; there is not even an appearance of danger ; and yet, if the whole depth below were one precipice, the effect could not be grander. At the foot is the cultivated valley, where the Glenderamaken, collecting the waters of Blencathra from the north and east, winds along to join St. John's Beck, and form with it the Greta. In front are the Ullswater mountains. The Vale of St. John's and Nathdale open into the subjacent valley ; you look over Nathdale fell, which divides them, and beyond it Leatheswater is seen, in its length, extending between Helvellyn and its own fells. Derwentwater is to the right of this, under the western side of those fells, and the semicircle is every where closed by mountains, range behind range. My friend, William Westall, who has seen the grandest and the loveliest features of nature in the East Indies and in the West, with the eye of a painter, and the feeling of a poet, burst into an exclamation of delight and wonder when I led him to this spot.

From Linthwaite Pike, which is the highest point of Blencathra, keeping along the brow, you pass in succession the points called Lilefell, Priestman and Knott Crag. They who
102

perform the whole excursion on foot, may descend from hence, in a south-westerly direction, to the Glenderaterra, cross that rivulet by a wooden bridge, and return to Keswick through Brundholm wood, by a very beautiful road, commanding views of the Greta in its manifold windings below, and, farther on, of the town, the lake, and the whole line of mountains from the Borrodale fells to Withop. But for women, and those from whom time has taken the superfluous strength of youth, it is better to be provided with carriages to the point where the ascent is commenced, and to rejoin them at the village of Threlkeld, descending, after they have passed Knott Crag, upon that village by a green shepherds' path. The path is not immediately perceptible from the heights, but, by making toward the village, you come upon it, and on so steep a declivity it is a great relief.

Threlkeld, when it is approached by the high road on either side, or from the Vale of St. John's, appears one of the least agreeable of our villages ; it presents no character of amenity or beauty, and seems rather to be threatened by the mountain, than sheltered by it. Very different is its appearance when you descend upon it from Highrow-fell by this green and pleasant path. Then, indeed, the village is beautiful ; not merely as a habitable human spot, the first which we reach upon issuing from some wild and uncultivated solitude, but in itself, and its position. The mountain, as thus seen, appears to protect and embosom it ; in front there is the little chapel to complete the picture, and sanctify, as it were, the scene ; and there is the musick of the mountain stream, accompanying the latter part of the descent, in unison with all the objects, and with the turn of mind which those objects induce.

GRASMERE (1830)

I WISH you could see Grasmere at this moment—the lake smooth as a silver shield for the most part, but freshen'd by partial currents of air which give relief and coolness to a somewhat sultry and electric atmosphere—one single boat rests on its oar or steals from one bass fishing spot to another. The woods are wearing now their darkest green, a hue less lovely to my eyes than the lustrous, transparent verdure of the spring.

So true is Wordsworth's observation (somebody has borrow'd my Wordsworth, and I'm like a Jack Tar without his tobacco pouch) that the older we grow, the more we become attach'd to things that typify Youth. Yet this ripe manhood of the year is beautiful still. The sun is shining bright, and yet there is a sombre tint in the air, that blends and modifies the lights and shades—the shadow'd clouds drag slowly over the mountain sides, and the smokes mount slowly as a solemn hymn to Heaven. Jupiter has been unusually pluvious with us—and the good folks are unromantically anxious about the hay day.

SUNSET AMONGST PRIMITIVE MOUNTAINS
(1833)

[The following passage is supposed to have been inspired by a walk up Great Gable.]

MOUNTAINS were not new to him; but rarely are Mountains seen in such combined majesty and grace as here. The rocks are of that sort called Primitive by the mineralogists, which always arrange themselves in masses of a rugged, gigantic character; which ruggedness, however, is here tempered by a singular airiness of form, and softness of environment: in a climate favourable to vegetation, the gray cliff, itself covered with lichens, shoots-up through a garment of foliage or verdure; and white, bright cottages, tree-shaded, cluster round the everlasting granite. In fine vicissitude, Beauty alternates with Grandeur: you ride through stony hollows, along strait passes, traversed by torrents, overhung by high walls of rock; now winding amid broken shaggy chasms, and huge fragments; now suddenly emerging into some emerald valley, where the streamlet collects itself into a Lake, and man has again found a fair dwelling, and it seems as if Peace had established herself in the bosom of Strength.

To Peace, however, in this vortex of existence, can the Son of Time not pretend: still less if some Spectre haunt him from the Past; and the Future is wholly a Stygian Darkness, spectre-bearing. Reasonably might the Wanderer exclaim to himself: Are not the gates of this world's Happiness inexorably shut against thee; hast thou a hope that is not mad? Nevertheless, one may still murmur audibly, or in the original Greek if that suit thee better: " Whoso can look on Death will start at no shadows."

From such meditations is the Wanderer's attention called outwards; for now the Valley closes-in abruptly, intersected by a huge mountain mass, the stony water-worn ascent of which is not to be accomplished on horseback. Arrived aloft, he finds himself again lifted into the evening sunset light; and cannot but pause, and gaze round him, some moments there. An upland irregular expanse of wold, where valleys in complex branchings are suddenly or slowly arranging their descent towards every quarter of the sky. The mountain-ranges are beneath your feet, and folded together: only the loftier summits look down here and there as on a second plain; lakes also lie clear and earnest in their solitude. No trace of man now visible; unless indeed it were he who fashioned that little visible link of Highway, here, as would seem, scaling the inaccessible, to unite Province with Province.

But sunwards, lo you! how it towers sheer up, a world of Mountains, the diadem and centre of the mountain region! A hundred and a hundred savage peaks, in the last light of Day; all glowing, of gold and amethyst, like giant spirits of the wilderness; there in their silence, in their solitude, even as on the night when Noah's Deluge first dried! Beautiful, nay solemn, was the sudden aspect to our Wanderer. He gazed over those stupendous masses with wonder, almost with longing desire; never till this hour had he known Nature, that she was One, that she was his Mother and divine. And as the ruddy glow was fading into clearness in the sky, and the Sun had now departed, a murmur of Eternity and Immensity, of Death and of Life, stole through his soul; and he felt as if Death and Life were one, as if the Earth were not dead, as if the Spirit of the Earth had its throne in that splendour, and his own Spirit were therewith holding communion.

SIR WALTER SCOTT AT THE LAKES
IN 1825 (1837)

THIS letter was written on the banks of Windermere, where we were received with the warmth of old friendship by Mr Wilson, and one whose grace and gentle goodness could have found no lovelier or fitter home than Elleray, except where she is now.

Mr Bolton's seat, to which Canning had invited Scott, is situated a couple of miles lower down on the same Lake; and thither Mr Wilson conducted him next day. A large company had been assembled there in honour of the Minister—it included already Mr Wordsworth and Mr Southey. It has not, I suppose, often happened to a plain English merchant, wholly the architect of his own fortunes, to entertain at one time a party embracing so many illustrious names. He was proud of his guests; they respected him, and honoured and loved each other; and it would have been difficult to say which star in the constellation shone with the brightest or the softest light. There was " high discourse ", intermingled with as gay flashings of courtly wit as ever Canning displayed; and a plentiful allowance, on all sides, of those airy transient pleasantries, in which the fancy of poets, however wise and grave, delights to run riot when they are sure not to be misunderstood. There were beautiful and accomplished women to adorn and enjoy this circle.

The weather was as Elysian as the scenery. There were brilliant cavalcades through the woods in the mornings, and delicious boatings on the Lake by moonlight; and the last day " the Admiral of the Lake " presided over one of the most splendid regattas that ever enlivened Windermere. Perhaps there were not fewer than fifty barges following in the Professor's radiant procession, when it paused at the point of Storrs to admit into the place of honour the vessel that carried kind and happy Mr Bolton and his guests. The three bards

107

of the Lakes led the cheers that hailed Scott and Canning ; and music and sunshine, flags, streamers, and gay dresses, the merry hum of voices, and the rapid splashing of innumerable oars, made up a dazzling mixture of sensations as the flotilla wound its way among the richy-folliaged islands, and along bays and promontories peopled with enthusiastic spectators.

On at last quitting the festive circle of Storrs, we visited the family of the late Bishop Watson at Calgarth, and Mr Wordsworth at his charming retreat of Mount Rydal. He accompanied us to Keswick, where we saw Mr Southey re-established in his unrivalled library. Mr Wordsworth and his daughter then turned with us, and passing over Kirkstone to Ulswater, conducted us first to his friend Mr Marshall's elegant villa, near Lyulph's Tower, and on the next day to the noble castle of his lifelong friend and patron Lord Lonsdale.

The Earl and Countess had their halls filled with another splendid circle of distinguished persons, who, like them, lavished all possible attentions and demonstrations of respect upon Sir Walter. He remained a couple of days, and perambulated, under Wordsworth's guidance, the superb terraces and groves of the " fair domain ", which that poet has connected with the noblest monument of his genius. But the temptations of Storrs and Lowther had cost more time than had been calculated upon, and the promised visit to Rokeby was unwillingly abandoned. Sir Walter reached Abbotsford again on the first of September, and said truly that " his tour had been one ovation."

THE MOUNTAIN COTTAGE—WESTMORELAND
(1838)

ONE of the principal charms of mountain scenery is its solitude. Now, just as silence is never perfect or deep without motion, solitude is never perfect without some vestige of life. Even desolation is not felt to be utter, unless in some slight degree interrupted : unless the cricket is chirping on the lonely hearth, or the vulture soaring over the field of corpses, or the one mourner lamenting over the red ruins of the devastated village, that devastation is not felt to be complete. The anathema of the prophet does not wholly leave the curse of loneliness upon the mighty city, until he tells us that " the satyr shall dance there ". And, if desolation, which is the destruction of life, cannot leave its impression perfect without some interruption, much less can solitude, which is only the absence of life, be felt without some contrast. Accordingly, it is, perhaps, never so perfect as when a populous and highly cultivated plain, immediately beneath, is visible through the rugged ravines, or over the cloudy summits of some tall, vast, and voiceless mountain.

When such a prospect is not attainable, one of the chief uses of the mountain cottage, paradoxical as the idea may appear, is to increase this sense of solitude. Now, as it will only do so when it is seen at a considerable distance, it is necessary that it should be visible, or, at least, that its presence should be indicated, over a considerable portion of surrounding space. It must not, therefore, be too much shaded by trees, or it will be useless ; but if, on the contrary, it be too conspicuous on the open hill side, it will be liable to most of the objections which were advanced against the Swiss cottage, and to another, which was not then noticed. Anything which, to the eye, is split into parts, appears less as a whole than what is undivided. Now, a considerable mass, of whatever tone or colour it may consist, is as easily divisible by dots as by lines ; that is, a conspicuous point, on any part of its surface, will divide it into two portions, each of which will be individually measured by the eye, but which will never make the impression which they would have made, had their unity not been interrupted. A conspicuous cottage on a distant mountain side has this effect in a fatal degree, and is, therefore, always intolerable.

It should accordingly, in order to reconcile the attainment of the good, with the avoidance of the evil, be barely visible : it should not tell as a cottage on the eye, though it should on the mind ; for be it observed that, if it is only by the closest investigation that we can ascertain it to be a human habitation, it will answer the purpose of increasing the solitude quite as well as if it were evidently so ; because this impression is produced by its appeal to the thoughts, not by its effect on the eye. Its colour, therefore, should be as nearly as possible that of the hill on which, or the crag beneath which, it is placed ; its form one that will incorporate well with the ground, and approach that of a large stone more than of anything else. The colour will consequently, if this rule be followed, be subdued and greyish, but rather warm ; and the form simple, graceful, and unpretending. The building should retain the same general character on a closer examination. Every thing about it should be natural, and should appear as if the influences and forces which were in operation around it had been too strong to be resisted, and had rendered all efforts of art to check their power, or conceal the evidence of their action, entirely unavailing. It cannot but be an alien child of the mountains ; but it must show that it has been adopted and cherished by them. This effect is only attainable by great ease of outline and variety of colour ; peculiarities which, as will be presently seen, the Westmoreland cottage possesses in a super-eminent degree.

Another feeling, with which one is impressed during a mountain ramble, is humility. I found fault with the insignificance of the Swiss cottage, because " it was not content to sink into a quiet corner, and personify humility ". Now, had it not been seen to be pretending, it would not have been felt to be insignificant; for the feelings would have been gratified with its submission to, and retirement from, the majesty of the destructive influences which it rather seemed to rise up against in mockery. Such pretension is especially to be avoided in the mountain cottage: it can never lie too humbly in the pastures of the valley, nor shrink too submissively into the hollows of the hills; it should seem to be asking the storm for mercy, and the mountain for protection: and should appear to owe to its weakness, rather than to its strength, that it is neither overwhelmed by the one, nor crushed by the other.

Such are the chief attributes, without which a mountain cottage cannot be said to be beautiful. It may possess others, which are desirable or objectionable, according to their situation, or other accidental circumstances. The nature of these will be best understood by examining an individual building. The material is, of course, what is most easily attainable and available without much labour. The Cumberland and Westmoreland hills are, in general, composed of clay-slate and grey-wacke, with occasional masses of chert (like that which forms the summit of Scawfell), porphyritic greenstone, and syenite. The chert decomposes deeply, and assumes a rough brown granular surface, deeply worn and furrowed. The clay-slate or grey-wacke, as it is shattered by frost, and carried down by torrents, of course forms itself into irregular flattish masses. The splintery edges of these are in some degree worn off by the action of water; and, slight decomposition taking place on the surface of the clay-slate, furnishes an aluminous soil, which is immediately taken advantage of by innumerable lichens, which change the dark grey of the original substance into an infinite variety of pale and warm colours.

These stones, thus shaped to his hand, are the most convenient building materials the peasant can obtain. He lays his foundation and strengthens his angles with large masses, filling up the intervals with pieces of a more moderate size; and using here and there a little cement to bind the whole together, and to keep the wind from getting through the interstices; but never enough to fill them altogether up, or to render the face of the wall smooth. At intervals of from

111

4 ft. to 6 ft. a horizontal line of flat and broad fragments is introduced projecting about a foot from the wall. Whether this is supposed to give strength, I know not; but as it is invariably covered by luxuriant stonecrop, it is always a delightful object.

The door is flanked and roofed by three large oblong sheets of grey rock, whose form seems not to be considered of the slightest consequence. Those which form the cheeks of the windows are generally selected with more care from the débris of some rock, which is naturally smooth and polished, after being subjected to the weather, such as granite or syenite. The window itself is narrow and deep set; in the better sort of cottages, latticed, but with no affectation of sweetbriar or eglantine about it. It may be observed of the whole of the cottage, that, though all is beautiful, nothing is pretty. The roof is rather flat, and covered with heavy fragments of the stone of which the walls are built, originally very loose; but generally cemented by accumulated soil, and bound together by houseleek, moss, and stonecrop: brilliant in colour, and singular in abundance.

It is well that, where every plant is wild and every torrent free, every field irregular in its form, every knoll various in its outline one is not startled by well built walls, or unyielding roofs, but is permitted to trace in the stones of the peasant's dwelling, as in the crags of the mountain side, no evidence of the line or the mallet, but the operation of eternal influences, the presence of an Almighty hand. Another perfection connected with its ease of outline is, its severity of character: there is no foppery about it; not the slightest effort at any kind of ornament, but what nature chooses to bestow; it wears all its decorations wildly, covering its nakedness, not with what the peasant may plant, but with what the winds may bring. There is no gay colour or neatness about it; no green shutters or other abomination: all is calm and quiet, and severe, as the mind of a philosopher, and, withal, a little sombre. It is evidently old, and has stood many trials in its day; and the snow, and the tempest, and the torrent have all spared it, and left it in its peace, with its grey head unbowed, and its early strength unbroken, even though the spirit of decay seems creeping, like the moss and the lichen, through the darkness of its crannies. This venerable and slightly melancholy character is the very soul of all its beauty.

There remains only one point to be noticed, its humility. This was before stated to be desirable, and it will here be found in perfection. The building draws as little attention upon itself as possible ; since, with all the praise I have bestowed upon it, it possesses not one point of beauty in which it is not equalled or excelled by every stone at the side of the road. It is small in size, simple in form, subdued in tone, easily concealed or overshadowed ; often actually so ; and one is always delighted and surprised to find that what courts attention so little is capable of sustaining it so well. Yet it has no appearance of weakness : it is stoutly, though rudely, built ; and one ceases to fear for its sake the violence of surrounding agencies, which, it may be seen, will be partly deprecated by its humility.

Such is the mountain cottage of Westmoreland ; and such, with occasional varieties, are many of the mountain cottages of England and Wales. It is true that my memory rests with peculiar pleasure in a certain quiet valley near Kirkstone, little known to the general tourist, distant from any public track, and, therefore, free from all the horrors of improvement : in which it seemed to me that the architecture of the cottage had attained a peculiar degree of perfection. But I think that this impression was rather produced by a few seemingly insignificant accompanying circumstances, than by any distinguished beauty of design in the cottages themselves. Their inhabitants were evidently poor, and apparently had not repaired their dwellings since their first erection ; and, certainly, had never torn one tuft of moss or fern from roofs or walls, which were green with the rich vegetation of years. The valley was narrow, and quiet, and deep, and shaded by reverend trees, among whose trunks the grey cottages looked out, with a perfection of effect which I never remember to have seen equalled, though I believe that, in many of the mountain districts of Britain, the peasant's domicile is erected with equal good taste.

GRETA HALL AND SOUTHEY (1839)

My dear Sara,

Here I am in the old dining room—which with the exception
of the original study is the least alter'd of any room about
the house. Well might Mother ask—what would Jacky and
Wilsy think could they rise again to see what work has been
made at Greta-Hall ! ! There is no need to say, considering
who has made it, that it is good work in the main, but nevertheless, it is melancholy work in my eyes. Perhaps it is partly
the weather, which is, as Uncle has call'd it half a dozen times,
rascally.

There is nothing sublime or satanic in its depravity—rascally
is the very word. Hard, harsh, uncomfortable, mirky frost-
melted rather than thaw'd by sleety rain—a patchy covering
of ragged-dirty snow—the mountains looking like great black
giants badly white-wash'd—the trees reduced by the late
tempest to more than wintry bareness—the ever greens, whose
verdure is always of a sombre cast, cold, grim, and rusty—
hardly one indication of approaching Spring at a time when
I have often seen the gardens all in a glow, the birds and
insects busy, the buds bursting with the pimply parturition of
vegetable life, the rathe primrose, and the starry celandine
" telling tales about the Sun ".

In plain speech, it is a very late season, and I can't help
thinking that the sky and the earth who are certainly in the
agricultural interest, are consumedly in the sulk at corn-law
agitation. I confess, I rather miss the uncarpeted vacancy of
Wilsy's parlour and Papa's study—though, they are furnished
with the best of all furniture, good books.

COTTAGE AT TROUTBECK

HAWKSHEAD IN WORDSWORTH'S SCHOOL-DAYS (1839)

ESTHWAITE, though a lovely scene in its summer garniture of woods, has no features of permanent grandeur to rely upon. A wet or gloomy day, even in summer, reduces it to little more than a wildish pond, surrounded by miniature hills : and the sole circumstances which restore the sense of a romantic region and an Alpine character are the towering groups of Langdale and Grasmere fells, which look over the little pastoral barriers of Esthwaite, from distances of eight, ten, and fourteen miles. Esthwaite, therefore, being no object for itself, and the sublime head of Coniston being accessible by a road which evades Hawkshead, few tourists ever trouble the repose of this little village town. And in the days of which I am speaking (1778–1787) tourists were as yet few and infrequent to *any* parts of the country.

Mrs. Radcliffe had not begun to cultivate the sense of the picturesque in her popular romances ; guidebooks, with the sole exception of *Gray's Posthumous Letters*, had not arisen to direct public attention to this domestic Calabria ; roads were rude, and, in many instances, not wide enough to admit post-chaises ; but, above all, the whole system of travelling accommodations was barbarous and antediluvian for the requisitions of the pampered south. As yet the land had rest ; the annual fever did not shake the very hills ; and (which was the happiest immunity of the whole) false taste, the pseudo-romantic rage, had not violated the most awful solitudes amongst the ancient hills by opera-house decorations. Wordsworth, therefore, enjoyed this labyrinth of valleys in a perfection that no one can have experienced since the opening of the present century. The whole was one paradise of virgin beauty ; the rare works of man, all over the land, were hoar with the grey tints of an antique picturesque ; nothing was new, nothing was raw and uncicatrized.

115

Hawkshead, in particular, though tamely seated in itself and its immediate purlieus, has a most fortunate and central locality, as regards the best (at least the most interesting) scenes for a pedestrian rambler. The gorgeous scenery of Borrowdale, the austere sublimities of Westdalehead, of Langdalehead, or Mardale—these are too oppressive, in their colossal proportions and their utter solitudes, for encouraging a perfectly human interest. Now, taking Hawkshead as a centre, with a radius of about eight miles, one might describe a little circular tract which embosoms a perfect network of little valleys—separate wards or cells, as it were, of one larger valley, walled in by the great leading mountains of the region. Grasmere, Easedale, Great and Little Langdale, Tilberthwaite, Yewdale, Elter Water, Loughrigg Tarn, Skelwith, and many other little quiet nooks, lie within a single division of this labyrinthine district. All these are within one summer afternoon's ramble. And amongst these, for the years of his boyhood, lay the daily excursions of Wordsworth.

AN EXCURSION OVER KIRKSTONE PASS IN 1807 (1839)

ON the third morning after my arrival in Grasmere, I found the whole family, except the two children, prepared for the expedition across the mountains. I had heard of no horses, and took it for granted that we were to walk ; however, at the moment of starting, a cart—the common farmers' cart of the country—made its appearance ; and the driver was a bonny young woman of the vale. Such a vehicle I had never in my life seen used for such a purpose ; but what was good enough for the Wordsworths was good enough for me ; and, accordingly, we were all carted along to the little town, or large village, of Ambleside—three and a half miles distant.

Our style of travelling occasioned no astonishment ; on the contrary, we met a smiling salutation wherever we appeared —Miss Wordsworth being, as I observed, the person most familiarly known of our party, and the one who took upon herself the whole expenses of the flying colloquies exchanged with stragglers on the road. What struck me with most astonishment, however, was the liberal manner of our fair driver, who made no scruple of taking a leap, with the reins in her hand, and seating herself dexterously upon the shafts (or, in Westmorland phrase, the *trams*) of the cart.

From Ambleside—and without one foot of intervening flat ground—begins to rise the famous ascent of Kirkstone ; after which, for three long miles, all riding in a cart drawn by one horse becomes impossible. The ascent is computed at three miles, but is, probably, a little more. In some parts it is almost frightfully steep ; for the road being only the original mountain track of shepherds, gradually widened and improved from age to age, (especially since the era of tourists began), is carried over ground which no engineer, even in alpine countries, would have viewed as practicable.

In ascending, this is felt chiefly as an obstruction and not

as a peril, unless where there is a risk of the horses backing ;
but in the reverse order, some of these precipitous descents
are terrific : and yet, once in utter darkness, after midnight,
and the darkness irradiated only by continual streams of
lightning, I was driven down this whole descent, at a full
gallop, by a young woman—the carriage being a light one, the
horses frightened, and the descents, at some critical parts of
the road, so literally like the sides of a house, that it was difficult
to keep the fore wheels from pressing upon the hind legs of
the horses. Indeed, this is only according to the custom of
the country, as I have before mentioned. The innkeeper of
Ambleside, or Lowwood, will not mount this formidable hill
without four horses. The leaders you are not required to take
beyond the first three miles ; but, of course, they are glad if
you will take them on the whole stage of nine miles, to Patterdale ; and, in that case, there is a real luxury at hand for those
who enjoy velocity of motion.

The descent into Patterdale is much above two miles ; but
such is the propensity for flying down hills in Westmoreland
that I have found the descent accomplished in about six
minutes, which is at the rate of eighteen miles an hour ; the
various turnings of the road making the speed much more
sensible to the traveller. The pass, at the summit of this
ascent, is nothing to be compared in sublimity with the pass
under the Great Gavil from Wastdalehead ; but it is solemn,
and profoundly impressive. At a height so awful as this, it
may be easily supposed that all human dwellings have been
long left behind : no sound of human life, no bells of churches
or chapels ever ascend so far.

On the solitary area of tableland which you find at the
summit—though, heaven knows, you might almost cover it
with a drawing-room carpet, so suddenly does the mountain
take to its old trick of precipitous descent, on both sides alike
—there are only two objects to remind you of man and his
workmanship. One is a guide-post—always a picturesque
and interesting object, because it expresses a wild country and
a labyrinth of roads, and often made much more interesting
(as in this case) by the lichens which cover it, and which record
118

the generations of men to whom it has done its office ; as also by the crucifix form which inevitably recall, in all mountainous regions, the crosses of Catholic lands, raised to the memory of wayfaring men who have perished by the hand of the assassin.

The other memorial of man is even more interesting :—Amongst the fragments of rock which lie in the confusion of a ruin on each side of the road, one there is which exceeds the rest in height, and which, in shape, presents a very close resemblance to a church. This lies to the left of the road as you are going from Ambleside ; and, from its name, Church-stone (Kirkstone,) is derived the name of the pass, and from the pass the name of the mountain. The guide-post—which was really the work of man—tells those going southwards (for to those who go northwards it is useless, since, in that direction, there is no choice of roads) that the left hand track conducts you to Troutbeck, and Bowness, and Kendal ; the right hand to Ambleside, and Hawkshead, and Ulverstone. The church—which is but a phantom of man's handiwork—might, however, really be mistaken for such, were it not that the rude and almost inaccessible state of the adjacent ground proclaims the truth. As to size, *that* is remarkably difficult to estimate upon wild heaths or mountain solitudes, where there are no leadings through gradations of distance, nor any artificial standards, from which height or breadth can be properly deduced.

This mimic church, however, has a peculiarly fine effect in this wild situation, which leaves so far below the tumults of this world ; the phantom church, by suggesting the phantom and evanescent image of a congregation, where never congregation met ; of the pealing organ, where never sound was heard except of wild natural notes, or else of the wind rushing through these mighty gates of everlasting rock—in this way, the fanciful image that accompanies the traveller on his road, for half a mile or more, serves to bring out the antagonist feeling of intense and awful solitude, which is the natural and presiding sentiment—the *religio loci*—that broods for ever over the romantic pass.

WESTMORELAND AUCTION SALES (1839)

IT is a custom, and a very ancient one, in Westmoreland—
the same custom (resting on the same causes) I have wit-
nessed also in southern Scotland—that any sale by auction of
household furniture (and seldom a month passes without
something of the sort) forms an excuse for the good women,
throughout the whole circumference of perhaps four or five
valleys, to assemble at the place of sale, with the nominal
purpose of buying something they may happen to want. A
sale, except it were of the sort exclusively interesting to farm-
ing *men*, is a kind of general intimation to the country, from
the owner of the property, that he will, on that afternoon, be
" at home " to all comers, and hopes to see as large an attendance as possible.

Accordingly, it was the almost invariable custom—and
often, too, when the parties were far too poor for such an
effort of hospitality—to make ample provision, not of eat-
ables, but of liquor, for all who came. Even a gentleman,
who should happen to present himself on such a festal occasion, by way of seeing the " humours " of the scene, was certain of meeting the most cordial welcome. The good woman
of the house more particularly testified her sense of the honour
done to her, and was sure to seek out some cherished and
solitary article of china—a wreck from a century back—in
order that he, being a porcelain man among so many delf men
and women, might have a porcelain cup to drink from.

The main secret of attraction at these sales—many of which
I have attended—was the social rendezvous thus effected
between parties so remote from each other (either by real
distance, or by virtual distance, resulting from the separation
effected by mountains 3000 feet high), that, in fact, without
some such common object, they would not be likely to hear
of each other for months, or actually to meet for years.

This principal charm of the " gathering," seasoned, doubtless, to many by the certain anticipation that the whole budget of rural gossip would then and there be opened, was not assuredly diminished to the men by the anticipation of excellent ale (usually brewed six or seven weeks before, in preparation for the event), and possibly of still more excellent *pow-sowdy* (a combination of ale, spirits, and spices) ; nor to the women by some prospect, not so inevitably fulfilled, but pretty certain in a liberal house, of communicating their news over excellent tea.

Even the auctioneer was always a character in the drama : he was always a rustic old humorist, and a jovial drunkard, privileged in certain good-humoured liberties and jokes with all bidders, gentle or simple, and furnished with an ancient inheritance of jests appropriate to the articles offered for sale —jests that had, doubtless, done their office from Elizabeth's golden days ; but no more, on that account, failing of their expected effect, with either man or woman of this nineteenth century, than the sun fails to gladden the heart, because it is that same old superannuated sun that has gladdened it for thousands of years.

Taken generally, however, these were the most picturesque and festal meetings which the manners of the country produced. There you saw all ages and both sexes assembled ; there you saw old men whose heads would have been studies for Guido ; there you saw the most colossal and stately figures amongst the young men that England has to show ; there the most beautiful young women. There it was that the social benevolence, the innocent mirth, and the neighbourly kindness of the people, most delightfully expanded, and expressed themselves with the least reserve.

THE KENDAL HIGHWAY BY NIGHT IN 1807 (1839)

THAT night, as I was passing under the grounds of Elleray, then belonging to a Westmoreland " statesman ", a thought struck me, that I was now traversing a road with which, as yet, I was scarcely at all acquainted, but which, in years to come, might perhaps be as familiar to my eye as the rooms of my own house ; and possibly that I might traverse them in company with faces as yet not even seen by me, but in those future years dearer than any which I had yet known.

In this prophetic glimpse there was nothing very marvellous ; for what could be more natural than that I should come to reside in the neighbourhood of the Wordsworths, and that this might lead to my forming connections in a country which I should consequently come to know so well ? I did not, however, anticipate so definitely and circumstantially as all this ; but generally I had a dim presentiment that here, on this very road, I should often pass, and in company that now, not even conjecturally delineated or drawn out of the utter darkness in which they were as yet reposing, would hereafter plant memories in my heart, the last that will fade from it in the hour of death.

Here, afterwards, at this very spot, or a little above it, but on this very estate, which, from local peculiarities of ground, and of sudden angles, was peculiarly *kenspeck, i.e.* easy of recognition, and could have been challenged and identified at any distance of years—here afterwards lived Professor Wilson, the only very intimate male friend I have had—here, too, it was, my M., that, in long years afterwards, through many a score of nights—nights often dark as Erebus, and amidst thunders and lightnings the most sublime—we descended at twelve, one, and two o'clock at night, speeding from Kendal to our distant home, twenty miles away. Thou wert at present a child not nine years old, nor had I seen thy face, nor heard thy name. But within nine years from that same night thou

122

wert seated by my side ;—and, thenceforwards, through a period of fourteen years, how often did we two descend, hand locked in hand, and thinking of things to come, at a pace of hurricane ; whilst all the sleeping woods about us re-echoed the uproar of trampling hoofs and groaning wheels.

Duly as we mounted the crest of Orrest Head, mechanically and of themselves almost, and spontaneously, without need of voice or spur, according to Westmoreland usage, the horses flew off into a gallop, like the pace of a swallow : it was a railroad pace that we ever maintained ; objects were descried far ahead in one moment, and in the next were crowding into the rear. Three miles and a half did this storm-flight continue, for so long the descent lasted. Then for many a mile, over undulating ground, did we ultimately creep and fly, until again a long precipitous movement, again a storm-gallop, that hardly suffered the feet to touch the ground, gave warning that we drew near to that beloved cottage ; warning to us—warning to them—

> The silence that is here
> Is of the grave, and of austere
> But happy feelings of the dead.

Sometimes the nights were bright with cloudless moonlight, and of that awful breathless quiet which often broods over vales that are peculiarly landlocked, and which is, or seems to be, so much more expressive of a solemn hush and a Sabbath-like rest from the labours of nature, than I remember to have experienced in flat countries :—

> It is not quiet—is not peace—
> But something deeper far than these.

And on such nights it was no sentimental refinement, but a sincere and hearty feeling, that, in wheeling past the village churchyard of Stavely, something like an outrage seemed offered to the sanctity of its graves, by the uproar of our career. Sometimes the nights were of that pitchy darkness which is more palpable and unfathomable wherever hills intercept the gleaming of light which otherwise is usually seen to linger about the horizon in the northern quarter; and then arose in perfection that striking effect, when the glare of lamps searches for one moment every dark recess of the thickets, forces them into sudden almost daylight revelation, only to leave them within the twinkling of the eye in darkness more profound; making them, like the snowflakes falling upon a cataract, " one moment bright, then gone for ever ". But, dark or moonlight alike, in every instance throughout so long a course of years, the road was entirely our own for the whole twenty miles.

After nine o'clock, not many people are abroad; after ten, absolutely none, upon the roads of Westmoreland; a circumstance which gives a peculiar solemnity to a traveller's route amongst these quiet valleys upon a summer evening of latter May, of June, or early July; since, in a latitude so much higher than that of London, broad day light prevails to an hour long after nine. Nowhere is the holiness of vesper hours more deeply felt.

THE NORTHERN LIGHTS FROM FOX HOW (1840)

I SOMETIMES think, that if I were at all in nervous spirits, the solemn beauty of this valley would be almost overwhelming, and that brick streets and common hedgerows would be better for me; just as now, whilst my life is necessarily so stirring, and my health so good, there is an extreme delight in the peacefulness of our life here, and in the quiet of all around us.

Last night we were out on the gravel walk for nearly half an hour, watching the northern lights. I never saw them so beautiful; the sky in the north behind the mountains was all of a silvery light, while in other parts it was dark as usual, and all set with its stars; then, from the mass of light before us, there shot up continually long white pillars or needles, reaching to the zenith; and then again fleeces of light would go quivering like a pulse all over the sky, till they died away in the far south. And today there is not a cloud to be seen, and the mountain before our windows reflects the sun's light upon us like a great mirror, we ourselves being in the shade, for the sun soon sets on this side of the valley. . . .

WINDERMERE AND THE FERRY (1842)

WINDERMERE! Why, at this blessed moment we behold the beauty of all its intermingling isles. There they are—all gazing down on their own reflected loveliness in the magic mirror of the airlike water, just as many a holy time we have seen them all agaze, when, with suspended oar and suspended breath—no sound but a ripple on the Naiad's bow, and a beating at our own heart—motionless in our own motionless bark—we seemed to float midway down that beautiful abyss between the heaven above and the heaven below, on some strange terrestrial scene composed of trees and the shadows of trees, by the imagination made indistinguishable to the eye, and as delight deepened into dreams, all lost at last, clouds, groves, water, air, sky, in their various and profound confusion of supernatural peace.

But a sea-born breeze is on Bowness Bay ; all at once the lake is blue as the sky : and that evanescent world is felt to have been but a vision. Like swans that had been asleep in the airless sunshine, lo ! where from every shady nook appear the white-sailed pinnaces ; for on merry Windermere—you must know—every breezy hour has its own Regatta.

There is not a prettier place on all Windermere than the Ferry-House, or one better adapted for a honey-moon. You can hand your bride into a boat almost out of the parlour window, and be off among the islands in a moment, or into nook or bay where no prying eye, even through telescope (a most unwarrantable instrument), can overlook your happiness ; or you can secrete yourselves, like buck and doe, among the lady-fern on Furness Fells, where not a sunbeam can intrude on your sacred privacy, and where you may melt down hours to moments, in chaste connubial bliss, brightening futurity with plans of domestic enjoyment, like long lines of lustre streaming across the lake. But at present, let us visit the fort-looking building among the cliffs called The Station,

ULLSWATER FROM GLENCOYNE WOOD

and see how Windermere looks as we front the east. Why, you would not know it to be the same lake.

The Isle called Beautiful, which heretofore had scarcely seemed an isle, appearing to belong to one or other shore of the mainland, from this point of view is an isle indeed, loading the lake with a weight of beauty, and giving it an ineffable character of richness which nowhere else does it possess ; while the other lesser isles, dropt " in nature's careless haste " between it and the Furness Fells, connect it still with those lovely shores from which it floats a short way apart, without being disunited one spirit blending the whole together within the compass of a fledgling's flight. Beyond these

> Sister isles, that smile
> Together like a happy family
> Of beauty and of love,

the eye meets the Rayrig woods, with but a gleam of water between, only visible in sunshine, and is gently conducted by them up the hills of Applethwaite, diversified with cultivated enclosures, " all green as emerald " to their very summits, with all their pastoral and arable grounds besprinkled with stately single trees, copses, or groves. On the nearer side of these hills is seen, stretching far off to other lofty regions— Hill-bell and High-street conspicuous over the rest—the long vale of Troutbeck, with its picturesque cottages, in " numbers without number numberless ", and all its sable pines and sycamores—on the further side, that most sylvan of all sylvan mountains, where lately the Hemans warbled her native wood-notes wild in her poetic bower, fitly called Dove-nest, and beyond, Kirkstone Fells and Rydal Head, magnificent giants looking westward to the Langdale Pikes (here unseen),

> The last that parley with the setting sun.

Immediately in front, the hills are low and lovely, sloping with gentle undulations down to the lake, here grove-girdled along all its shores. The elm-grove that overshadows the Parsonage is especially conspicuous—stately and solemn in a green old age—and though now silent, in spring and early summer clamorous with rooks in love or alarm, an ancient family, and not to be expelled from their hereditary seats.

Following the line of shore to the right, and turning your eyes unwillingly away from the bright and breezy Belsfield, they fall on the elegant architecture of Storr's Hall, gleaming from a glade in the thick woods, and still looking southward they see a serene series of the same forest scenery, along the heights of Gillhead and Gummer's-How, till Windermere is lost, apparently narrowed into a river, beyond Townhead and Fellfoot, where the prospect is closed by a beaconed eminence clothed with shadowy trees to the very base of the Tower.

The points and promontories jutting into the lake from these and the opposite shores—which are of a humbler, though not tame character—are all placed most felicitously; and as the lights and shadows keep shifting on the water, assume endless varieties of relative position to the eye, so that often during one short hour you might think you had been gazing on Windermere with a kaleidoscopical eye, that had seemed to create the beauty which in good truth is floating there for ever on the bosom of nature.

FROM BOWNESS TO TROUTBECK (1842)

IT is about a Scottish mile, we should think, from Bowness Cook's House—along the turnpike road—half the distance lying embowered in the Rayrig woods—and half open to lake, cloud, and sky. It is pleasant to lose sight now and then of the lake along whose banks you are travelling, especially if during separation you become a Druid. The water woos you at your return with her bluest smile, and her whitest murmur.

Some of the finest trees in all the Rayrig woods have had the good sense to grow by the roadside, where they can see all that is passing—and make their own observations on us deciduous plants. Few of them seem to be very old—not much older than Christopher North—and, like him, they wear well, trunk sound to the core, arms with a long sweep, and head in fine proportions of cerebral development, fortified against all storms—perfect pictures of oaks in their prime. You may see one—without looking for it—near a farmhouse called Miller-ground—himself a grove. His trunk is clothed in a tunic of moss, which shows the ancient Sylvan to great advantage, and it would be no easy matter to give him a fall.

Should you wish to see Windermere in all her glory, you have but to enter a gate a few yards on this side of his shade, and ascend an eminence called by us Greenbank—but you had as well leave your red mantle in the carriage, for an enormous white, long-horned Lancashire bull has for some years established his head-quarters not far off, and you would not wish your wife to become a widow, and with six fatherless children. But the royal road of poetry is often the most splendid—and by keeping the turnpike, you soon find yourself on a terrace to which there was nothing to compare in the hanging gardens of Babylon. There is the widest breadth of water—the richest foreground of wood—and the most magnificent background of mountains—not only in Westmorland but—believe us—in all the world.

That blue roof is Calgarth—and no traveller ever pauses on this brow without giving it a blessing—for the sake of the illustrious dead; for there long dwelt in the body Richard Watson, the Defender of the Faith, and there within the shadow of his memory still dwell those dearest on earth to his beatified spirit. So pass along in high and solemn thought, till you lose sight of Calgarth in the lone road that leads by St Catharine's, and then relapse into pleasant fancies and picturesque dreams.

This is the best way by far of approaching Troutbeck. No ups and downs in this life were ever more enlivening—not even the ups and downs of a bird learning to fly. Sheep-fences, six feet high, are admirable contrivances for shutting out scenery; and by shutting out much scenery, why, you confer an unappreciable value on the little that remains visible, and feel as if you could hug it to your heart. But sometimes one does feel tempted to shove down a few roods of intercepting stone-wall higher than the horsehair on a cuirassier's casque—though sheep should eat the suckers and scions, protected as they there shoot, at the price of the concealment of the picturesque and the poetical from beauty-searching eyes.

That is a long lane, it is said, which has never a turning; so this must be a short one, which has a hundred. You have turned your back on Windermere—and our advice to you is, to keep your face to the mountains. Troutbeck is a jewel—a diamond of a stream—but Bobbin Mills have exhausted some of the most lustrous pools, changing them into shallows, where the minnows rove. Deep dells are his delight—and he loves the rugged scaurs that intrench his wooded banks—and the fantastic rocks that tower-like hang at intervals over his winding course, and seem sometimes to block it up; but the miner works his way out beneath galleries and arches in the living stone—sometimes silent—sometimes singing—and sometimes roaring like thunder—till subsiding into a placid spirit, ere he reaches the wooden bridge in the bonny holms of Calgarth, he glides graceful as the swan that sometimes sees his image in his breast, and through alder and willow banks murmurs away his life in the Lake.

130

Yes—that is Troutbeck Chapel—one of the smallest and to our eyes the very simplest—of all the chapels among the hills. Yet will it be remembered when more pretending edifices are forgotten—just like some mild, sensible, but perhaps somewhat too silent person, whose acquaintanceship—nay, friendship—we feel a wish to cultivate we scarce know why, except that he is mild, sensible, and silent ; whereas we would not be civil to the *brusque*, upsetting, and loquacious puppy at his elbow, whose information is as various as it is profound, were one word or look of courtesy to save him from the flames.

For Heaven's sake, Louisa, don't sketch Troutbeck Chapel. There is nothing but a square tower—a horizontal roof—and some perpendicular walls. The outlines of the mountains here have no specific character. That bridge is but a poor feature—and the stream here very commonplace. Put them not on paper. Yet alive—is not the secluded scene felt to be most beautiful ? It has a soul. The pure spirit of the pastoral age is breathing here—in this utter noiselessness there is the oblivion of all turmoil ; and as the bleating of flocks comes on the ear, along the fine air, from the green pastures of the Kentmere range of soft undulating hills, the stilled heart whispers to itself, " this is peace ! "

The worst of it is, that of all the people that on earth do dwell, your Troutbeck *statesmen*, we have heard, are the most litigious—the most quarrelsome about straws. Not a footpath in all the parish that has not cost many pounds in lawsuits. The most insignificant style is referred to a full bench of magistrates. That gate was carried to the Quarter Sessions. No branch of a tree can shoot six inches over a march-wall without being indicted for a trespass. And should a frost-loosened stone tumble from some *skrees* down upon a neighbour's field, he will be served with a notice to quit before next morning.

Many of the small properties hereabouts have been mortgaged over head and ears mainly to fee attorneys. Yet the last hoop of apples will go the same road—and the statesman, driven at last from his paternal fields, will sue for something or another *in forma pauperis*, were it but the worthless wood and second-hand nails that may be destined for his coffin. This is a pretty picture of pastoral life—but we must take pastoral life as we find it. Nor have we any doubt that things were every whit as bad in the time of the patriarchs—else— whence the satirical sneer, " sham Abraham " ?

Yonder is the village straggling away up along the hill-side, till the furthest house seems a rock fallen with trees from the mountain. The cottages stand for the most part in clusters of twos and threes—with here and there what in Scotland we should call a *clachan*—many a sma' toun within the ae lang toun ; but where in all braid Scotland is a mile-long scattered congregation of rural dwellings, all dropt down where the Painter and the Poet would have wished to plant them, on knolls and in dells, and on banks and braes, and below tree-crested rocks, and all bound together in picturesque confusion by old groves of ash, oak, and sycamore, and by flower-gardens and fruit-orchards, rich as those of the Hesperides ?

THE ASCENT OF FAIRFIELD (1855)

STILL further on, when the sheep are all left behind, the stranger may see a hawk perched upon a great boulder. He will see it take flight when he comes near, and cleave the air below him, and hang above him—to the infinite terror, as he knows, of many a small creature there—and then whirl away to some distant part of the park. Perhaps a heavy buzzard may rise, flapping from her nest on the moor, or pounce from a crag in the direction of any water-birds that may be about the springs and pools in the hills. There is no sound, unless it be the hum of the gnats in the hot sunshine.

There is an aged man in the district, however, who hears more than this, and sees more than people would, perhaps, imagine. An old shepherd has the charge of four water-gauges which are set up on four ridges—desolate, misty spots, sometimes below but often above the clouds. He visits each once a month, and notes down what the gauges record ; and when the tall old man, with his staff, passes out of sight into the cloud, or among the cresting rocks, it is a striking thought that science has set up a tabernacle in these wildernesses, and formed a priest among the shepherds.

That old man has seen and heard wonderful things ; has trod upon rainbows, and been waited upon by a dim retinue of spectral mists. He has seen the hail and the lightnings go forth as from under his hand ; and has stood in the sunshine listening to the thunder growling and the tempest bursting beneath his feet. He well knows the silence of the hills, and all the solemn ways in which that silence is broken.

The stranger, however, coming hither on a calm summer-day, may well fancy that a silence like this can never be broken.

Looking abroad, what does he see ? The first impression probably is the billowy character of the mountain groups around and below him. This is perhaps the most striking

133

scene to a novice ; and the next is, the flitting character of the mists. One ghostly peak after another seems to rise out of its shroud ; and then the shroud winds itself round another. Here the mist floats over the valley ; there it reeks out of a chasm ; here it rests upon a green slope ; there it curls up a black precipice. The sunny vales below look like a paradise, with their bright meadows and waters, and shadowy woods and little knots of villages.

To the south there is the glittering sea ; and the estuaries of the Leven and the Duddon, with their stretches of yellow sands. To the east, there is a sea of hill-tops. On the north, Ullswater appears, grey and calm at the foot of the black precipices ; and nearer may be traced the whole pass from Patterdale, where Brothers' Water lies invisible from hence. The finest point of the whole excursion is about the middle of the *cul-de-sac*, where, on the northern side, there are tremendous precipices overlooking Deepdale and other sweet recesses far below.

Here, within hearing of the torrents which tumble from those precipices, the rover should rest. He will see nothing so fine as the contrast of this northern view with the long green slope on the other side, down to the source of Rydal Beck, and then down to Rydal Woods and Mount ; but, the further he goes, the more amazed he will be at the extent of the walk, which looked such a trifle from below. He is now 2,745 feet above the sea-level ; and he has surely earned his meal.

THE ASCENT OF CARROCK (1857)

WITHOUT a word of inquiry, therefore, the Two Idle Apprentices drifted out resignedly into a fine, soft, close, drowsy, penetrating rain : got into the landlord's light dog-cart, and rattled off through the village for the foot of Carrock. The journey at the outset was not remarkable. The Cumberland road went up and down like all other roads ; the Cumberland curs burst out from the backs of cottages and barked like other curs ; and the Cumberland peasantry stared after the dog-cart amazedly, as long as it was in sight, like the rest of their race.

The approach to the foot of the mountain resembled the approaches to the feet of most other mountains all over the world. The cultivation gradually ceased, the trees grew gradually rare, the road became gradually rougher, and the sides of the mountain looked gradually more and more lofty, and more and more difficult to get up. The dog-cart was left at a lonely farm-house. The landlord borrowed a large umbrella, and, assuming in an instant the character of the most cheerful and adventurous of guides, led the way to the ascent.

Mr. Goodchild looked eagerly at the top of the mountain, and, feeling apparently that he was now going to be very lazy indeed, shone all over wonderfully to the eye, under the influence of the contentment within and the moisture without. Only in the bosom of Mr. Thomas Idle did Despondency now hold her gloomy state. He kept it a secret ; but he would have given a very handsome sum, when the ascent began, to have been back again at the inn.

The sides of Carrock looked fearfully steep, and the top of Carrock was hidden in mist. The rain was falling faster and faster. The knees of Mr. Idle—always weak on walking excursions—shivered and shook with fear and damp. The wet was already penetrating through the young man's outer

135

coat to a brand-new shooting-jacket, for which he had reluct-
antly paid the large sum of two guineas on leaving town ; he
had no stimulating refreshment about him but a small packet
of clammy gingerbread nuts ; he had nobody to give him an
arm, nobody to push him gently behind, nobody to pull him
up tenderly in front, nobody to speak to who really felt the
difficulties of the ascent, the dampness of the rain, the dense-
ness of the mist, and the unutterable folly of climbing,
undriven, up any steep place in the world, when there is level
ground within reach to walk on instead.

Was it for this that Thomas had left London ? London,
where there are nice short walks in level public gardens, with
benches of repose set up at convenient distances for weary
travellers—London, where rugged stone is humanely pounded
into little lumps for the road, and intelligently shaped into
smooth slabs for the pavement ! No ! it was not for the
laborious ascent of the crags of Carrock that Idle had left his
native city, and travelled to Cumberland. Never did he feel
more disastrously convinced that he had committed a very
grave error in judgment than when he found himself standing
in the rain at the bottom of a steep mountain, and knew that
the responsibility rested on his weak shoulders of actually
getting to the top of it.

The honest landlord went first, the beaming Goodchild
followed, the mournful Idle brought up the rear. From time
to time the two foremost members of the expedition changed
places in the order of the march ; but the rearguard never
altered his positon. Up the mountain and down the mountain, in the water or out of it, over the rocks, through the
bogs, skirting the heather, Mr. Thomas Idle was always the
last, and was always the man who had to be looked after and
waited for.

At first the ascent was delusively easy, the sides of the
mountain sloped gradually, and the material of which they
were composed was a soft spongy turf, very tender and pleasant
to walk upon. After a hundred yards or so, however, the
verdant scene and the easy slope disappeared, and the rocks
began. Not noble, massive rocks, standing upright, keeping

a certain regularity in their positions, and possessing, now and then, flat tops to sit upon, but little, irritating, comfortless rocks, littered about anyhow by Nature; treacherous, disheartening rocks of all sorts of small shapes and small sizes, bruisers of tender toes and trippers-up of wavering feet.

When these impediments were passed, heather and slough followed. Here the steepness of the ascent was slightly mitigated; and here the exploring party of three turned round to look at the view about them. The scene of the moorland and the fields was like a feeble water-colour drawing half sponged out. The mist was darkening, the fields were all getting blurred together, and the lonely farm-house where the dog-cart had been left, loomed spectral in the grey light like the last human dwelling at the end of the habitable world. Was this a sight worth climbing to see? Surely—surely not!

Up again—for the top of Carrock is not reached yet. The landlord, just as good-tempered and obliging as he was at the bottom of the mountain. Mr. Goodchild brighter in the eyes and rosier in the face than ever; full of cheerful remarks and apt quotations; and walking with a springiness of step wonderful to behold. Mr. Idle, farther and farther in the rear, with the water squeaking in the toes of his boots, with his two-guinea shooting-jacket clinging damply to his aching sides, with his overcoat so full of rain, and standing out so pyramidically stiff, in consequence, from his shoulders downwards that he felt as if he was walking in a gigantic extinguisher—the despairing spirit within him representing but too aptly the candle that had just been put out.

Up and up and up again, till a ridge is reached and the outer edge of the mist on the summit of Carrock is darkly and drizzingly near. Is this the top? No, nothing like the top. It is an aggravating peculiarity of all mountains, that, although they have only one top when they are seen (as they ought always to be seen) from below, they turn out to have a perfect eruption of false tops whenever the traveller is sufficiently ill-advised to go out of his way for the purpose of ascending them. Carrock is but a trumpery little mountain of fifteen hundred feet, and it presumes to have false tops, and even precipices, as if it were Mont Blanc. No matter ; Goodchild enjoys it, and will go on : and Idle, who is afraid of being left behind by himself, must follow.

On entering the edge of the mist, the landlord stops, and says he hopes that it will not get any thicker. It is twenty years since he last ascended Carrock, and it is barely possible, if the mist increases, that the party may be lost on the mountain. Goodchild hears this dreadful intimation, and is not in the least impressed by it. He marches for the top that is never to be found, as if he was the Wandering Jew, bound to go on for ever, in defiance of everything. The landlord faithfully accompanies him. The two, to the dim eye of Idle, far below, look in the exaggerative mist, like a pair of friendly giants, mounting the steps of some invisible castle together. Up and up, and then down a little, and then up, and then along a strip of level ground, and then up again.

The wind, a wind unknown in the happy valley, blows keen and strong : the rainmist gets impenetrable ; a dreary little cairn of stones appears. The landlord adds one to the heap, first walking all round the cairn, as if he were about to perform an incantation, then dropping the stone on to the top of the heap with the gesture of a magician adding an ingredient to a cauldron in full bubble. Goodchild sits down by the cairn as if it was his study-table at home : Idle, drenched and panting, stands up with his back to the wind, ascertains distinctly that this is the top at last, looks round with all the little curiosity that is left in him, and gets, in return, a magnificent view of—Nothing !

COCKLEY BECK (1861)

WE began to think that Cockley Beck ought to be near, and yet there was no visible habitation in the silent glen. At last we spied a shepherd stalking along the hill with a lame sheep on his shoulders ; and a clump of stunted trees came in sight, by the streamlet side. Our path led up to the trees, and we found a rude farmstead partly sheltered by them. It certainly didn't look promising at first. Could this be Cockley Beck that we had heard of so oft ? We knocked, and inquired. The good-wife came to the door, and said, with a smile, " This is t'pleeace. There's neea udder hoose i't daal. Will ye cum in ? " We sat down in a low-roofed room, at the front.

The smoky rafters were hung with hams, and shrunken legs of cured mutton ; and, on a long shelf near the ceiling there were little cheeses, dried herbs, staves, jars, and a tattered book or two. By the ingle, a tall, grey-haired man, in clogs, corduroy breeches, and a rough light-blue woollen jacket, of home-made cloth, was quietly watching the wood fire, and keeping it up by laying sticks on from a pile before him.

He was eighty-three years of age, and very deaf. Stealing a look at us occasionally, he turned away again, and went on feeding the fire, with a countenance as calm as if he were a statue of contented age. Evening was drawing on, and they told us we could stay all night, so we doffed our satchels, and began to be at home. The good-wife bustled about in her blue bedgown ; and a low babble of children came from a room behind, which was half-filled with eilding for the winter. Looking out at the window, on the other side of the narrow vale, Hardknot rose bleak and craggy to the skies. Between its summit and that of Harter Fell, a lofty pass leads into Eskdale. About halfway down the Eskdale side are the ruins of a Roman camp, called Hardknot Castle, " whose guardians bent the knee to Jove and Mars ". In the opening between

Hardknot and Wrynose, Scawfell was pointed out, " with a lile mist a-top on it ".

There was about an hour and a half of daylight left ; and, as it was " nobbut a mile an' a hauf, mebby ", to Hardknot Castle, we agreed to go there whilst tea was preparing. It was strange to see a little girl of thirteen put on her best clothes to go with us as guide. The sun had set before we reached the head of the pass, and the wind blew keen across.

The ruins lie about half-way down the opposite side—a great square of fallen stones, on a commanding platform, looking over Eskdale out to the sea—a very beautiful prospect. Around the ruins mighty mountains frowned, Scawfell, Hardknot, and Harter Fell, all savage desolation. That wild scene must have changed very little since Roman trumpets woke its echoes. Scawfell saw those warriors come and go, like the mists on his summit ; and he still looks proudly upon their scattered camp, untameable by aught but Him who reared his head so high. We had only a few minutes to wander in this ruined eyrie of the Roman eagle. The shades of evening were making green Eskdale dim, and we hastened up the pass again.

By the time we reached John Tyson's house, candles were burning inside ; clouds were gathering gloomily, and it began to rain. A white cloth was on the table, and a bright wood fire filled the room with ruddy light. The goodwife spread our board with ham and eggs, and steaks of cured mutton ; brown bread, white bread, and spice cakes ; cheese, preserves, strong tea, and cream—such as cities seldom get to see. John Tyson had come in from the fells, and he sat on a long wood bench under the window, very quiet. A great sheep-dog lay asleep on the hearth. It had a stony look about the eyes, and I thought it old, and perhaps blind.

Cockley Beck was rushing by the front of the house, and the wind and rain filled the lone glen with a wild roaring. Sitting comfortably by the solitary farmer's fire, there was a strange charm in listening to the elementary war that raged in darkness around us. By way of getting into talk, I asked Tyson how old the dog was. He said it was only three years
140

old. Dogs didn't last so long among those fells. They had a hard life of it. We noticed the wood fire ; and he told us that brush-wood and turf was all they had to burn. Coals were too far off, and would cost too much for carriage.

" What," said he, " we're verra nee oot o' t' warld, ye see ; for Cocklo' Beck's seb'm mile fra a mill, five mile fra a shop, an' aboon fower mile fra a church—an' hard roads tull it, as ye'll hev sin." He said they made their own candles of the pith of rushes dipped in mutton fat. They made as many in two days as lasted the whole year. These rush dips are not much thicker than a strong knitting-needle, and give but a dreary light to people accustomed to gas. But they seemed to think the light very good : beside, they went to bed very soon o' nights.

An iron clip, something like a pair of curling tongs, hung from the ceiling by a string ; and in this clip the rushlight was stuck aslant, and shifted as it burnt away. Leather for the family's shoes was bought whilst at market, in Broughton or Whitehaven ; and the shoes were made in their own house, by a wandering son of Crispin, who went from farm to farm among the fells, getting his meat and lodging, and, as I understood, about two shillings a pair, for his work.

It was the same with clothing. A tailor came up the glen at certain times, and folding his legs upon the long table under the window for a few days, he ate and drank with the rest, and chatted and stitched away, till they were clothed for the year. Being among such a way of life as this felt like living three hundred years ago ; and, somehow, the place reminded me of the highland bothy at Aberfoyle, where Bailie Nichol Jarvic singed the chieftain's tartan with a red hot poker.

UP THE DUDDON (1864)

THEN on again, having now lost the river within the rocks until you pass Wallabarrow, when there it is again, beautiful as ever, under the crags, the birds singing in the trees, and the cows pasturing in the fields—a perfect picture of peace and sweetness, till you come to a greenish-grey lane which leads you down to some stepping-stones. Not the famous stones ; only a few " water-teeth " for the shepherds, where, however, you may stand and see the grandeur of the rift—a sheer chasm where the water rushes in unchecked force, the fell all in gold and purpled tones, while isolated crags come out in cool grey, and the background of wild mountains of a deep bloomy purple. A very noticeable bit this of the Duddon ; perhaps the loveliest and most noticeable of all, with the stormy river rushing so fiercely forward to bury itself, like many a life too eager and too passionate, within the depths of the rock, and behind the gates of death and bondage. Only, with no eternity of death for the river, as so often for the life ; for the rock gates open again beyond, and the Duddon strides through them into the light of life and the joy of the sun once more, for many a long and lovely mile before its last issue into the waste of waters by Duddon Sands.

A long dale, and a wild one, this which you are now traversing, uninhabited save at rare intervals, when you fall upon a few poor fell-side dwellings ; at least not fall upon them, for oftentimes they are off the line of such " high road " as it is, and well-nigh inaccessible at certain seasons and in certain weathers ; but great is the courage of the dalesmen, and wonderful their powers of isolation, sustaining, as they so often do, a life of almost unbroken solitude, with minds not uncultivated, and manners not rude if less than soft. They form a race apart, and are the most interesting of the mountain folk. But wild and lonely as this dale is, how full of incident ! Here you come to Goldrill Crag and Wordsworth's Fairy

Chasm, where the roots of the rock are of a pure blue below the water, though only of a warm dove-colour in the sunlight; where the water is no longer a river but a broken cascade; and where the wild fells, backed by the wilder mountains—Harter Fell and Birker Fell on the one side, the Old Man and Wetherlam and Walna Scar on the other, Wrynose and Grey Friars in front—seem the very term of all human life.

DOWN TO THE LAKE AT KESWICK (1871)

THE night had fallen already when I reached the water-side, at a place where many pleasure-boats are moored and ready for hire ; and as I went along a stony path, between wood and water, a strong wind blew in gusts from the far end of the lake. The sky was covered with flying scud ; and, as this was ragged, there was quite a wild chase of shadow and moon-glimpse over the surface of the shuddering water. I had to hold my hat on, and was growing rather tired, and inclined to go back in disgust, when a little incident occurred to break the tedium. A sudden and violent squall of wind sundered the low underwood, and at the same time there came one of those brief discharges of moonlight, which leaped into the opening thus made, and showed me three girls in the prettiest flutter and disorder. It was as though they had sprung out of the ground.

I accosted them very politely in my capacity of stranger, and requested to be told the names of all manner of hills and woods and places that I did not wish to know, and we stood together for a while and had an amusing little talk. The wind, too, made himself of the party, brought the colour into their faces, and gave them enough to do to repress their drapery ; and one of them, amid much giggling, had to pirouette round and round upon her toes (as girls do) when some specially strong gust had got the advantage over her. They were just high enough up in the social order not to be afraid to speak to a gentleman ; and just low enough to feel a little tremor, a nervous consciousness of wrong-doing—of stolen waters, that gave a considerable zest to our most inno-cent interview. They were as much discomposed and flut-tered, indeed, as if I had been a wicked baron proposing to elope with the whole trio ; but they showed no inclination to go away, and I had managed to get them off hills and waterfalls and on to more promising subjects, when a young

144

RAW HEAD, LANGDALE

man was descried coming along the path from the direction of Keswick.

Now whether he was the young man of one of my friends, or the brother of one of them, or indeed the brother of all, I do not know ; but they incontinently said that they must be going, and went away up the path with friendly salutations. I need not say that I found the lake and the moonlight rather dull after their departure, and speedily found my way back to potted herrings and whisky-and-water in the commercial room with my late fellow-traveller.

In the smoking-room there was a tall dark man with a moustache, in an ulster coat, who had got the best place and was monopolising most of the talk ; and, as I came in, a whisper came round to me from both sides, that this was the manager of a London theatre. The presence of such a man was a great event for Keswick, and I must own that the manager showed himself equal to his position. He had a large fat pocket-book, from which he produced poem after poem, written on the backs of letters or hotel-bills ; and nothing could be more humorous than his recitation of these elegant extracts, except perhaps the anecdotes with which he varied the entertainment. Seeing, I suppose, something less countrified in my appearance than in most of the company, he singled me out to corroborate some statements as to the depravity and vice of the aristocracy, and when he went on to describe some gilded saloon experiences, I am proud to say that he honoured my sagacity with one little covert wink before a second time appealing to me for confirmation. The wink was not thrown away ; I went in up to the elbows with the manager, until I think that some of the glory of that great man settled by reflection upon me, and that I was as noticeably the second person in the smoking-room as he was the first. For a young man, this was a position of some distinction, I think you will admit. . . .

AGAINST THE EXTENSION OF RAILWAYS IN THE LAKE DISTRICT (1876)

SUPPOSE I were sitting, where still, in much changed Oxford, I am happy to find myself, in one of the little latticed cells of the Bodleian Library :—and my kind and much loved friend, Mr. Coxe, were to come to me, with news that it was proposed to send nine hundred excursionists through the library every day, in three parties of three hundred each :—that it was intended they should elevate their minds by reading all the books they could lay hold of while they stayed ;—and that practically scientific persons accompanying them were to look out for, and burn, all the manuscripts that had any gold in their illuminations, that the said gold might be made of practical service :—but that he, Mr. Coxe, could not, for his part, sympathize with the movement, and hoped I would write something in deprecation of it !

As I should then feel, I feel now, at Mr. Somervell's request that I would write him a preface in defence of Helvellyn. What could I say for Mr. Coxe ? Of course, that nine hundred people should see the Library daily, instead of one, is only fair to the nine hundred, and if there is gold in the books, is it not public property ? If there is copper or slate in Helvellyn, shall not the public burn or hammer it out—and they say they will, of course—in spite of us ?

What does it signify to *them* how we poor old quiet readers in this mountain library feel ? True, we know well enough, —what the nine hundred excursionist scholars don't—that the library can't be read quite through in a quarter of an hour ; also, that there is a pleasure in real reading, quite different from that of turning pages ; and that gold in a missal, or slate in a crag, may be more precious than in a bank, or a chimney pot. But how are these practical people to credit us—these, who cannot read, nor ever will ; and who have been taught
146

that nothing is virtuous but care for their bellies, and nothing useful but what goes into them?

Whether to be credited or not, the real facts of the matter, made clear as they are in the following pages, can be briefly stated for the consideration of any candid person.

The arguments in favour of the new railway are in the main four, and may be thus answered.

I. "There are mineral treasures in the district capable of development."

Answer. It is a wicked fiction, got up by whosoever has got it up, simply to cheat shareholders. Every lead and copper vein in Cumberland has been known for centuries; the copper of Coniston does not pay; and there is none so rich in Helvellyn. And the main central volcanic rocks, through which the track lies, produce neither slate nor hæmatite, while there is enough of them at Llanberis and Dalton to roof and iron grate all England into one vast Bedlam, if it honestly perceives itself in need of that accommodation.

II. "The scenery must be made accessible to the public."

Answer. It is more than accessible already;—the public are pitched into it head-foremost, and necessarily miss two-thirds of it. The Lake scenery really begins, on the south, at Lancaster, where the Cumberland hills are seen over More-cambe Bay; on the north, at Carlisle, where the moors of Skiddaw are seen over the rich plains between them and the Solway. No one who loves mountains would lose a step of the approach, from these distances, on either side. But the stupid herds of modern tourists let themselves be emptied, like coals from a sack, at Windermere and Keswick. Having got there, what the new railway has to do is to shovel those who have come to Keswick, to Windermere—and to shovel those who have come to Windermere, to Keswick. And what then?

III. "But cheap, and swift transit is necessary for the working population, who otherwise could not see the scenery at all."

Answer. After all your shrieking about what the operatives spend in drink, can't you teach them to save enough out of

147

their year's wages to pay for a chaise and pony for a day, to drive Missis and the Baby that pleasant 20 miles, stopping when they like, to unpack the basket on a mossy bank? If they can't enjoy the scenery that way—they can't any way; and all that your railroad company can do for them is only to open taverns and skittle grounds round Grasmere, which will soon, then, be nothing but a pool of drainage, with a beach of broken gingerbeer bottles; and their minds will be no more improved by contemplating the scenery of such a lake than of Blackpool.

IV. What else is to be said? I protest I can find nothing, unless that engineers and contractors must live. Let them live; but in a more useful and honourable way than by keeping Old Bartholomew Fair under Helvellyn, and making a steam merry-go-round of the lake country.

There are roads to be mended, where the parish will not mend them, harbours of refuge needed, where our deck-loaded ships are in helpless danger : get your commissions and dividends where you know that work is needed; not where the best you can do is to persuade pleasure-seekers into giddier idleness.

WINTER CLIMBS (1894)

ONLY a few years ago a man who announced that he was going to the Lakes in the depth of winter would have been thought mad. Exclamations of this kind are even now not unfrequently called forth at that season of the year ; yet they seem to have little or no effect in diminishing the number of those who year by year find themselves somehow attracted to the little inns which lie at the foot of Snowdon or of Scafell Pikes.

On Swiss mountains winter excursions have been made even by ladies, and perhaps the British public was first rendered familiar with the idea of by Mrs Burnaby's book on the subject. But, in truth, the invention is no new one, and those bold innovators who first dared to break through the pale of custom and to visit North Wales or the Lakes in mid-winter were richly repaid for their audacity ; for there is hardly any time of the year at which a trip to Lakeland is more thoroughly enjoyable.

In the first place, there is no crowd. You can be sure that you will get a bed, and that the people of the house will not be, as they too often are in the summer time, too much over-worked to have time to make you comfortable, or too full of custom to care much whether you are comfortable or not. Out of doors there is the same delightful difference. You stride cheerily along, freed for a time from the din of toiling cities, and are not harassed at every turn by howling herds of unappreciative " trippers ". The few who do meet on the mountains are all bent on the same errand and " mean business " ; half-hearted folk who have not quite made up their minds whether they care for the mountains or not, people who come to the Lakes for fashion's sake, or just to be able to say that they have been there, are snugly at home coddling themselves before the fire. You will have no companions but life-long lovers of the mountains, and robust young fellows whose highest ambition is to gain admission to the Alpine Club, or, having gained it, to learn to wield with some appearance of dexterity the ponderous ice-axes which are indispensable to the dignity of their position. Then what views are to be had through the clear, frosty air !

How different are the firm outlines of those distant peaks from the hazy indistinctness which usually falls to the lot of the summer tourist ! What sensation is more delightful than that of tramping along while the crisp snow crunches under foot, and gazing upward at the lean black crags standing boldly out from the long smooth slopes of dazzling white ! There is no great variety of colour ; for the rocks, though a few are reddish, are for the most part of grey in varying shades ; yet there is no monotony.

It is true that January days have one fault ; they are too short. Or shall we not rather say that they seem so because —like youth, like life itself—they are delightful ? They would not be too short if they were passed (let us say) in breaking stones by the roadside. After all, the hills hereabouts are not so big but that in eight or nine hours of brisk exertion a very satisfactory day's work can be accomplished. In short, youth and strength (and no one can be said to have left these behind who can still derive enjoyment from a winter's day on the Fells) can hardly find a more delightful way of spending a week of fine frosty weather.

FROM AMBLESIDE TO GRASMERE (1902)

THE valley of Ambleside, with its wooded knolls of rock standing among the grass, and Loughrigg looking down, shadowy and solemn ; and the sudden turn to new scenery when you come to Rydalwater, very dainty with its fringy shores and islets—to use the old word, " smiling " under the frown of Nab Scar ; and then the new surprise, swiftly following, of Grasmere, whether you take the low road by the lake shore, or the old road over the hill, or the middle road by the spot where the Wishing Gate used to be, Grasmere under Silver How, as shadowy as Loughrigg, and still more solemn, and the water's face untroubled, and the island-hillock severe in outline, pensive and lonely ; then in a few minutes again another scene—the opening dale, and the great masses of the mountains lifting up their lines from it in one huge heave together, shoulder to shoulder, and the splintered crest of Helm Crag and the multitudinous heights behind it, over against Helvellyn—it is rarely that so much beauty is crowded into so little ground. And if you take the well-known walks —Greenhead Gill where " Michael " built his sheep-fold, Tongue Gill and its waterfall, or up to Grisedale Tarn—Greenburn behind the Helm, or Easedale with its tarn and force, or any of the gills along the breast of wooded Silver How— " custom cannot stale their infinite variety ". Wordsworth chose well.

CONISTON WATER, PAST AND PRESENT
(1902)

BUT Coniston Water is a singular instance of nature's *vis medicatrix*, the way she heals old sores. Along the beach and in every little dell where an unfailing streamlet runs down, there used to be iron furnaces (bloomeries), where small charges of ore, brought on pack-horses and boats from Low Furness, were smelted with charcoal. At one time the woods were nearly destroyed, and we can imagine a period when the barren hills were only varied by smoking " pitsteads ", where charcoal was made, and flaming " hearths " where grimy workers toiled at the bellows, or shovelled the red ore and black coals, with shouts and rattling, and the thud of the little water-wheels that worked the hammers and drove the blast.

Perhaps not all the scene was at any one time so filled, but that was the character of the place. And now there is no such dainty frondage and foliage, no such utter peace and stillness, as in the coves and crannies of the water's edge, where softly rowing you may start the otter and the kingfisher, and hear no noise but the splash of the leaping trout, and the distinguishable call of many streams—this one tinkling, that one gurgling, and one beyond belling through the woods, and another across half a mile of water chattering over the stones or roaring down its coppice-hidden ravine.

UPPER ESKDALE AND THE SCAFELLS (1902)

HENCE upwards, Eskdale is a glorious wilderness. Dungeon Gill and Wasdale-head Hotels are the nearest houses, five miles as the crow flies, but with Bowfell in the way of the one and Scafell in the way of the other : due north it is more than six miles in a bee-line to Seathwaite in Borrowdale over Esk Hause. You can play at being lost, and imagine a great lone land ; yet the heights and distances are only big enough to give the illusion for a few hours' ramble, and you are sure—barring accidents—to come down somewhere into civilisation before nightfall.

We have no other bit of wild country like this, and hitherto it has not been spoiled for the purposes of a playground by too much meddling. A very little pathmaking and setting up of signposts would take away the charm of finding your own road, of attacking Nature single-handed, which is the thing that gives our homeland an advantage over more stupendous Alps, where you must take a guide, not to say more extensive mountain tracts where you cannot go without a whole caravan.

At Esk Force the valley branches : that to the right leads up to Bowfell, or over the Ure Gap to Langstrath ; that to the left leads up to the grand inner valley, which is walled by the crags of Scafell, the Pikes, and Great End, successively emerging, each more impressive than the last. Continuing up the valley, you reach Esk Hause, and meet the track between Styhead and Rossett Gill.

Sprinkling Tarn and Angle Tarn, though they are set among crags like the tarns of Coniston, are curiously different from them in their situation. Instead of occupying the bottoms of coves, combes, or corries, they are perched on watershed ridges. This is not uncommonly the case with rock basins too small to be called tarns, but here the peculiar structure occurs on a considerable scale, and with circumstances of scenery which make it not easily forgotten. On a cloudless,

153

hot day, perhaps, when one is tired and thirsty, and the sun glares into every cranny of the rocks, cutting up the scene into weariful spottiness, one may pass this way without uplifting of soul.

But let the mountains have something to talk about; let them dress up in their clouds or their snows, and act their parts : show what they can do with white dazzle against blue and black, or give you peeps of distant lake vignetted like a Turner sketch, or hints of crag behind crag and crest above crest, and now and then a swirl of grey, trailing over green tarn-banks and valley bottoms, lifting its curtain on new scenes, of which there is an inexhaustible store—for the mist has every sort of transformation trick ready ; it is Nature's own stage-manager—and then you will see the drama of mountain gloom and mountain glory.

Possibly, if it is so minded, the sun may help, and throw blazing searchlights on green and gold and lilac, or dewy rainbows, or even the rare fogbow, with your shadow in the centre, the true Brocken Spectre ; possibly, climbing higher still, as you follow the frequent cairns that lead to the topmost cairn of the Pikes, you may feel the blue overhead penetrating the vapour, and suddenly stand above a waving sea of opalescence, with islands of hardly recognisable peaks blocked on the silent void.

I have seen these things when folk below were kicking their heels and grumbling at the weather ; but even if there is nothing but rain and rain, with a map and a compass, and some habit of mountain walking—without which the fear of being lost overbalances the pleasure—even then there is a delight in wandering here, through the heart of the hills, far beyond the easy amusements of sunny roads and lake shores.

The two separate mountains of Scafell and the Scafell Pikes are like two castle towers, between which would be a clear course but for a little gatehouse filling the gap. The gatehouse has a ridged roof, one end of which rests against the side of each tower. The northern tower, Scafell Pikes, has been so battered at the top that you can clamber down its ruined upper storey and get upon the ridge of the gatehouse roof. Then you are in Mickledore, the great gap; but when you have " ridden the rough roofbeam ", like an Icelandic ghost, and reach the other side, thinking to climb the southern tower, Scafell, you find that it is not nearly so ruined. Indeed, it stands up with pinnacles and buttresses so high, and flanking precipices so deep, and even in places overhanging, that here, if anywhere in these mountains, one can get the impression of size and awesomeness which the usual quiet contour and un-exciting altitudes cannot give.

Right in front of Mickledore ridge the blocky volcanic-ash formation cleaves into a set of giant steps, as it were tilted from behind, so that the top of each step slopes outwards, and what should be vertical often overhangs. That is the Broad Stand, accessible a little to the left of the ridge; but it needs a long arm, or, better still, a friend to give you a lift. Farther to the left is the Chimney, easy to climb for some distance, but near the top the trouble begins; and if you are not accus-tomed to climbing, the return from this point is dangerous.

To the right of the ridge is the Lord's Rake, a gully which is the least difficult of the three routes to the top. There have been misadventures enough on this perilous edge to warn inexperienced wanderers to leave it alone. As a matter of scenery, the best points of view are from the other and safer side of Mickledore. Scafell can be climbed without risk from south or east or west; it is only this face that needs Alpine gymnastics; and when you are at the cairn on the Pikes you are at the highest point in England, without the danger of this lower summit.

SMALL WATER (1905)

MY first glimpse of Small Water was at sunset. Afternoon was far spent when we faced the mountain ways. Along the hilltops the sun flashed golden fire, the fells to eastward were haloed in bright mist, cool shadows fell and spread around. Then after an (it seemed interminable) hour, we came here. Not a spark of direct light fell into the hollow of the hills, but the waters shook off responsive glows to day's aftermath reigning in the skies. The air was hushed, the wagtails flittering about the grey stones were soothed to cuttering monotones.

Oh, to stay were glorious indeed, to watch the now radiant vault fade through most subtle hues to grey and then to clear blue of night and starry rest. But on we had to go—often the most ravishing scene has to be inexorably hurried through, for man has many interests, and the most peaceful, the most soul-filling, are not in the way of the world the most important. Would that more of us could, like the poets whose dreamings inspired the mighty deeds of old, and of today as well, sit by the hour in these realms of beauty and delight, and calmly let their spirit sink into us. We would write better, live better ; but what we call duty intervenes and the inner pulsations of living nature remain unknowable.

Nature as seen indoors with the microscope is unfolded to us every day by our great leaders of thought ; but few of these great minds care for or have the leisure to instil into themselves, and thence transmit to us, the broader splendours of field and fell and mere.

A SUNRISE FROM HELVELLYN (1906)

OUT west, the hills that when we began to ascend from Grasmere were levelled by the mist, are now clear of cloudy film, and assert themselves in bold individuality. First and foremost the Great Gable stands up huge—the Pillar mountain behind him but, away to the south-west, Bowfell and Crinkle Crags melt into Greyfriars and Wetherlam—a wall of slaty blue—and Coniston Old Man shows clear against the glimmer of the sea.

Now furious blows the wind ; the grasses rustle and rise and fall beneath the blast. We turn our backs upon it, and are almost blown along towards the gate in the iron wire fence that seems so out of place on such a height. One mutters to oneself that the age of Neolithic man and his stone wall cunning is better far than this degenerate age of iron and barbed wire, and passing through it, we gain welcome shelter from the wind, and so coast along below the ridge of the bluff, till on a sudden we find ourselves at the precipice edge, and hear the wind singing in the crags and thundering at the black walls of the Dolly-Waggon bastion that face the east.

Down far below us, like a grey silver thread, a stream, fed by a thousand springs, flows to Patterdale, then wanders out of sight, and the deep trough of Grisedale is laced from side to side with tributary streams that flow to join the main beck and pass to Ullswater. But the great charm of the view lies in that long uneven crescent of light between Place Fell and distant Gowbarrow, which, piercing the distant grey and blue of encircling hills and woods and meadows, lies bare of bosom to the morn. So still, so beautiful, it lies, that we, in the fortress tower of the winds forget the " business of the elements ", and feel the peace of Ulph's-water possess our hearts.

And now black clouds that hung in a mellow sea of amber fire, changed from blackest grey, from grey to violet, from violet to rose, and the white fleeces of the cloud flocks in

157

heaven were smitten into gold as they wandered to the west. The bastions, jetty black below our feet, went gold green. Such miracle of power had that far-off giant of life as to change the grey grass into verdure, and the iron blackness and mist into golden beauty ; but the lake changed not. Motionless, impassive, it gave no response to the morning's call, and out west for the next thirty minutes it seemed as if the mountains cared not for the day.

But as we gazed backward, the grass imperceptibly had changed colour at our feet, and the great buttress of Seat Sandal glimmered and glowed as with a hidden flame ; while over the purple hollows and the grey-blue wilderness of Armboth and High Whitestones we saw how, through the gap of Grisedale, the peaks that lay with vision and touch of the as yet unlifted sun, gleamed into russet gold, and kindled to the dawn. The light of saffron was now on the further hills, the light of lemon-yellow faintly flickered to the zenith, and right across the saffron sky, above the Pennine Range— so blue, so grey, there was laid bar upon bar of rosy fiery cloud, as if some giant had been forging in a vast forge, or drawing from some red-hot furnace, the pillars of a vast pavilion or mighty throne against the coming of a king.

Then as we watched, making all the landscape darker for his advent, we saw above Crossfell a ruby jewel burn—a jewel first in lozenge shape that grew to semicircle, and at last, almost as it seemed with a bound, leapt up a perfect disk above the hills. So making the winds his chariot and coming forth from his pavilion as a giant to run his course, the great sun came, and all the far-off hills and vales were glad because of him. Suddenly, as if at the word of his command, a thousand angels in bright-bannered beauty sped as couriers from before his face. Now first we heard the bleating of the mountain sheep, now first we saw the bleaberry flash into emerald green, and while the raven swung out from the crag and barked above us, the stone-chat cracked his stones together and bobbed from grey to white.

It is a very different matter going down a mountainside in clear light and ascending it in semi-darkness, and in less than an hour we found ourselves at the intake gate above Tongue Ghyll; in another thirty minutes we had entered the village, where, though the sun was bright on roof and field, the villagers still slept, and only here and there a blue puff of wood smoke from a distant fellside farm, told that the mountain shepherd was awake. Two sunrises were ours to-day.

We had seen the sun rise like a rosy jewel on the Crossfell Range, and as we swung to the garden gate at Grasmere that morning, we saw him once more rise in glowing might above the larch trees of Buthar's Crag, the eastern rampart of the vale.

SKATING ON DERWENTWATER (1913)

I KNEW that to-morrow, if the wind kept in the east, the ice on Derwentwater would be in prime condition, and having much work to do, I also knew that there would be no skating for me unless rising betimes I could go off by star and moonlight to the lake. At five-thirty I was astir. Great silver clouds built up the heights of nobler mountains in the south, but westward the moon shone in a cloudless sky. Leaving the quiet house and passing through the sleeping hamlet and through the little town, which, but for light in three windows and in the pencil factory, was still asleep, I made my way to the " lands ", and as the clock struck six—the only living thing in that strange landscape—I shod myself with steel and struck out from the land.

Orion had sunk beneath the western hills ; the Plough was at the zenith. I knew that three morning stars were rejoicing together to run their course, but one was not yet visible above the hills, the other was dimmed by the moonlight that seemed to wash the heaven clear of stars, save where Cassiopeia still sparkled faintly above Skiddaw and Jupiter, rejoicing in his strength and glory, yet shone clear above Scafell, and as I saw it gleam in the polished ice I could not help thinking of how Wordsworth years ago on Esthwaite Lake had seen just such reflection of a planet when he " cut across the reflex of a star ".

The weirdness of the scene lay in the fact that all the near hills seemed blackened as though the breath of a great fire had passed over them and left behind white ash and ebon darkness. The woods about the lake appeared to have grown in density. One might have supposed Derwentwater stood in a huge forest ; in the dim moonlight the dark woods seemed so magnified in mass. There was no sound of life except bark of dog from the neighbouring town, and the calling of the owls to one another across the lake. There was no sight of
160

SKATING ON DERWENTWATER

life except that in two or three places in the dense woodland a bright lamp shone that told us that the busy servants of the household were awake.

It was poorish skating, for though brooms had been busy on Saturday, the ice had been much cut by skates, and on beyond this broomland the snow of Thursday last lay in patches. The skates rustled through the snow and rang upon the clear ice spaces, and the cold air from the east an hour before the dawn, made one's face and ears tingle as one pressed against it. As for the moon, she must have been discomforted to think that all her desire to build a golden pillar upon the shining surface of the mere was foiled by these continued snow patches, which broke up the building of her glory into sections of gold, and dimness of dusky silver.

But on beyond the white snow patches lay what looked at first in the dim twilight like open water. It was not till I was close above it that I found this open water a solid sheet of ebon ice without a wrinkle in it. I do not know how it is, but the feeling of " The Ancient Mariner " comes back upon us all when we are the first to burst into an untravelled world, whether it be a sea, a desert waste, or a sheet of ice, and one could not help a sense of thrill with moon and stars alone to be one's companions. I hissed across that wonderful ice-sheet, swerving and curving with a new sense of power and unaccustomed speed, with Jupiter bright in the mirror before me and the great moon pillar of gold across my way, till, out of breath and with the blood racing warm through my heart, I leaned upon my heels and let the wind carry me where it would.

Weird and mysterious as had been the moonlit time, the coming of the dawn upon the ice-sheet and surrounding fells was more marvellously wonderful. What a colourist the sun-god is ! The dark woods changed to amber brown far upon the slopes of Skiddaw, the bracken sent its fire from beneath the snow, and slowly the ebon blackness between its cone of snow passed into puce and violet purple, as if beneath some enchanter's wand.

The gulls went greyly like ghosts overhead ; silent without

L

cawing, a black swarm of rooks passed from Lord's Island to their hard work afield of food-finding for the day. They knew the moon must pale and the sun must grow, and that ere they reached their far-off feeding ground the light would be given them for their difficult task. But the joylessness with which the black-winged multitude passed touched me deeply. The frost might give me pleasure, but would give them pain.

Suddenly the cup of the sky to the east was flushed as with new wine. The great solid bars of crimsoning seemed melted into liquid amber till it flushed and flushed again. The mackerel sky overhead seemed in a moment to become a great flight of rosy-winged flamingoes flying to the west, and a faint cloud above the Wanthwaite heights took on gorgeous colour from the rose of dawn.

But the beauty was not in heaven but upon the shining ebon floor of the lake. Its dark blackness disappeared, and in a moment the vast ice-sheet became first green, then gold, and then of rosy hue. Involuntarily I pulled up and gazed upon the wonder thus revealed, and as I gazed the wonder grew and grew. The moon was still shining above Hindscarth, the sun had not yet appeared, but all her light had paled before the coming of the day, and all the mystery of the heavens was forgotten in the marvel of that polished floor of rose and gold ingrain.

It is good to skate at noon and eventide. It is better far to skate when moon and starlight fade before the dawn.

THROUGH THE WOODS TO SAWREY (1929)

UP hill and down hill, Pony Billy trotted on and on; and the woods stretched mile after mile. The tall, straight tree-trunks gleamed in white ranks; trees in hundreds of thousands. Pony Billy glanced skeerily right and left. Almost he seemed to hear phantom galloping horseshoes, as his own shoes pattered on the road. Almost he seemed to see again the fairy dancers of Mettle's story by the forge.

Shadows of a shadow! Was that the shadow of a little hooded figure, flitting across a forest ride? and a dark prowling shadow that followed her? Was the trotting shadow on the road beside him the shadow of himself? Or was it the shadow of another pony? A little bay pony in a pony trap, with an old woman and a bob-tailed dog, caught in a snowstorm in the woods?

But this white road was not white with snow; and they were real overtaking footsteps that caused Pony Billy to spring forward with a start of panic. Three roe-deer cantered by. Their little black hoofs scarcely touched the ground, so lightly they bounded along. They made playful grunting noises, and dared Pony Billy to catch them; he arched his neck and trotted his best, while he " hinnied " in answer to the deer. They bore him merry company for longer than a mile; sometimes gambolling alongside; sometimes cantering on before.

On and on they travelled; through many miles of woods. Past the black firs; past the sele bushes in the swamp; past the big beech trees; uphill and down. Sometimes a rabbit darted across their path. And once they saw two strange dwarfy figures crossing the road in front of them—stumpy, waddling figures, broad as they were long; running, running. The second trundled a handbarrow; the foremost pulled it with a rope—there go the Oakmen! Are those pissamoor hills in the glade? or are they tiny charcoal settings on the pit-steads? The gambolling roe-deer kick up their heels.

They know the weight of Oakman Huddikin's sledge in
winter ! But this is spring. The dwarfy red-capped figures,
running like two little fat badgers, disappeared in the moonlight behind the Great Oak.

At length the woods grew thinner. There began to be
moonlit clearings ; small parrocks where the Big Folk last
summer had hung white streamers on sticks, to scare the red
stags from the potato drills. The friendly roe-deer turned
aside and left him, leaping a roadside fence, with a flicker of
white scuts.

Pony Billy by himself reached a lonely farmsteading ; he
was pleasantly warm after his long brisk trot. He turned up
a narrow yard between manure heaps and a high stone building,
that showed a white-washed front to the moon. He passed
the doors of byres. Sleepy cows mooed softly ; their warm
sweet breath smelled through the door-slats. A ring-widdie
clinked, as a cow turned her head to listen to the wheels.

Pony Billy passed several more doors. Old Tiny, the sow,
was snoring peacefully behind one of them. He drew the
cart round the end of the shippon into a cobble-paved yard,
where the wheels rumbled over the stones. He went up to the
back door of the house. There was no light upstairs ; the
window panes twinkled in the moonlight. A faint red glow
showed through the kitchen window and under the back door.

Mary Ellen, the farm cat, sat within ; purring gently, and
staring at the hot white ashes on the open hearth ; wood ash
that burns low, but never dies for years. She sat on a dun-
coloured deer-skin, spread on the kitchen flags. Pots and
pans, buckets, firewood, coppy stools, cumbered the floor, and
a great brown cream mug was set to warm before the hearth
against the morrow's churning. The half-stone weight belonging to the butter scales was on the board that covered the mug ;
Mary Ellen had not been sampling the cream. She sat before
the hot wood ash and purred. Crickets were chirping. All
else was asleep in the silent house.

SCAFELL CRAG

PRESERVATION OF THE SCENERY (1929)

OUR scenery is not like that of Switzerland. The Alps are so huge that their glories can long defy the assaults even of modern machinery. But it would be easy to destroy the beauty of our little Lake District. Two or three motor roads in certain places, one of them over Wrynose and another over the famous Sty Head, with big hotels on the pass tops and red villas and bungalows spotted over the valley heads below, would go far to complete the destruction of that still incomparable region. And common English scenery, whether of the Home Counties, of the South-West or of the Midlands, is a delicate and fugitive beauty, made up of small touches, a combination of nature with the older arts of man in a harmony which can be easily destroyed by a few rash strokes of the crude levelling machinery of modern life.

Why is it worth while to be at expense and trouble to preserve some at least of these natural beauties of England?

The most obvious reason is the lowest—the financial. Nowadays natural beauty has its price. The visitors to England, particularly the Americans, come to taste the garden-like enchantment of this green island, which has not its like in the grand and spacious scenery of their own continent. If we spoil our island, their descendants will have the less inducement to visit it. And, just as the natural beauty of the island is a financial asset and a source of distinction to the nation as a whole, so the natural beauty of each shire and region is a source of wealth and honour to the local inhabitants. If the men of Devon or of Surrey allow the peculiar charm of their county to be destroyed for a little immediate advantage to individuals, they will as a community be bad men of business. The city dweller longs for natural beauty of which he has been deprived at home, and seeks it out on his holiday. To attract him where he can find it and to cater for him there is a great legitimate trade. But in order that it should flourish, natural beauty must be preserved, if only as a business asset.

The inhabitants of some districts seem inclined to kill the goose that lays the golden eggs, by building right on the top of their most beautiful places. The type of house built and the precise situation of the house in a beautiful region are matters of common concern. If a man plants an ugly building where it injures the landscape, he is impoverishing the neighbourhood.

But it is not merely, it is not even chiefly, a matter of money. The happiness and the soul's health of the whole people are at stake. The preservation of natural beauty as an element in our nation's life is a cause that deeply concerns people of every sort who are working to maintain any ideal standards and any healthy life. The world of religion in all its branches, the world of education, the patriot, the social reformer, the lover of old times, the lovers of literature and poetry, the artists and musicians, the bird-lovers and zoologists, all have the strongest possible motives to forget all feuds in common support of this cause. They give it too little attention, for if natural beauty disappears, religion, education, national tradition, social reform, literature and art, will all be deprived of a principal source of life and vigour that in our island has helped them immeasurably in the past and is helping them still.

Without vision the people perish, and without natural beauty the English people will perish in the spiritual sense. In old days the English lived in the midst of nature, subject to its influence at every hour. Thus inspired our ancestors produced their great creations in religion, in song, and in the arts and crafts—common products of a whole people spiritually alive. Today most of us are banished to the cities, not without deleterious effects on imagination, inspiration, and creative power. But some still live in the country and some still come out on holidays to the country, to drink in with the zest of the thirsty man the delights of natural beauty, and return to the town re-invigorated in soul.

STONE WALLS (1929)

A LEARNED tome might well be written on the subject of stone walls at the Lakes, and a good deal has been written in this book and that. It seems that the first stone walls at the Lakes were built in prehistoric days when the Neolithic inhabitants began to give up their wigwams and a more or less nomadic way of life and took to living in hamlets of stone huts or isolated stone farmsteads, and enclosing little fields for themselves within stone walls. Here, in the north-west, though it gradually shifted down into the dales, settlement of this type persisted, with each of the scattered farms and hamlets possessing its own little enclosures, so that some of the existing fence walls, though periodically rebuilt, may perpetuate the outlines of fields walled in when the dales were reclaimed from wood and marsh.

Where stones were scarce and the soil of sufficient depth hedges or dykes were used instead of walls, and in mediaeval days, once the boundaries of properties ceased to be defined by reference to striking natural objects like " the white stone in Little Greenop ", or as " beginning at the top of the rock which stands in the ditch above the oak " dykes were often built, like that made in 1279, to keep Grasmere cattle from trespassing in the deer forest of Rydal. Here, a wall appears to have been built from Rydal Water up Nab Scar and to have been continued as a ditch and bank, remains of which are still visible along the ridge beyond.

At the head of Eskdale the monks of Furness Abbey had permission about 1290 to enclose some thirty acres of pasture, near Butterilket, with a " dyke, wall, or paling " such as the deer of the adjoining forest of Egremont could leap. They chose to build a dyke, of earth and stone, and this is still in existence though a more recent fence has been made more or less parallel with it.

For wooden fences the native woods supplied plenty of

material. Hedgerows of young, growing trees, half cut through and trained to grow horizontally, in a few years formed, as they do still, a dense partition, while light fences of hurdles, easily removable, were used to enclose the growing hay crops of such little communities as thirteenth-century Ambleside. The limits of cultivated lands not requiring such protection were sometimes defined by " mear stones ", and at Ambleside an old reference to the " wall Yeat " seems to show that walls, and hence gates in them, were then so uncommon as to be sufficiently defined by such a description.

The manor of Baisbrown was partly enclosed by a hedge, and it is recorded that the ancient bounds of the manor of Coniston followed in places a hedge : " and so upwards by the hedge which parts the several Allans belonging to Yewdale from Furness Fell grounds ". The tenants in Ennerdale promised in 1560 to " inclose their grounds severally with quycksetts according to the poyntment of the statute ", and eight years later it was recognised that they ought to enclose their grounds with " quicksets " at their own charges. And in Langdale today, as in other dale bottoms, hedges as well as dry stone walls form the irregular, wandering boundaries of the fields so that in autumn the vivid green of the little grass-lands is beautifully criss-crossed by the red and gold of hedgerow trees, and in winter the bare top-most stems are etched in a delicate, hairlike tracery against the grey-white of the frozen pastures. . . .

On higher ground where, above the dales, there was less woodland, a soil too thin to grow lusty hedges, stones often strewn about in plenty and no house-building to compete for their use, walls were built even on Furness Fells, noted in early days for their forests, tenants were directed in the time of Henry VIII that their enclosures from the common land were " to be hedged with dyke or wall ". Most of the fell walls of today, however, date back to the enclosures that were made in the latter part of the eighteenth century and the earlier half of the nineteenth. Indeed, the course of recent agri-cultural history at the Lakes has been marked by the gradual extension of walls, in a stony spider's web of hundreds of miles of stone fences, over the fell slopes; still more recent history is reflected in their slow decay.

Until comparatively modern times at the Lakes, the fells were open common land and only with their enclosure came into being that familiar network of dark stone fences, covering all but the higher slopes, that is now accepted as a characteristic, and even beloved, part of the Lake Country landscape. Incidentally it is interesting to wonder what societies for the preservation of Lakeland scenery would have said about the building of these walls, had such societies then existed. Often enough they run up to the skyline, climbing the steepest slopes as if they had the power of clinging to the land, like the wall up Nab Scar above Rydal, and those on the green fells that rise so abruptly from the valley of the Westmorland Troutbeck. They cross grassy slopes so steep and bare, like those of Stone Arthur at Grasmere, that the stones for the walls must have been carried up by horse-drawn sledges.

There are walls running up crags, as on the fells east of Rosthwaite in Borrowdale; walls enclosing fell-side lanes, the bulges and contractions of which lanes have been determined by the outline of the areas enclosed on either side; walls surrounding intakes of every conceivable shape, of which the older ones, to be seen on Naddle Fell, Silverhow, Rydal Fell and almost everywhere, are said to be marked by a rounded upper bulge, since it was easier to build a wall without corners, and in the early days no one cared particularly how much or how little was enclosed from the common fell. And so, more or less between the years of 1760 and 1820, happy farmers at the Lakes, with roads and railways beginning to open to them the markets of industrial England and bringing in all kind of new agricultural ideas, fashioned the fantastic pattern of stone walls upon the Lake Country hill-sides.

THE CHANGING SEASONS (1929)

MOREOVER, in the Lake Country the changing seasons not only alter the whole face of the landscape, not only divide the dalesfolk's year into two periods, the tourist season and the non-tourist season, but also advance and retreat themselves in so leisurely and apparently erratic a manner as to draw the attention of the least observant to the mysteries of their annual progress. Here the state of the season is not only a matter concerned with the sun and the latitude : here the fells take a hand in the astronomical game, and what with their varying heights, the shadows they cast, and the way they face or turn their slopes from the sun, introduce an infinite complexity into the changing of the seasons.

The Wasdale Head mountains, seen from the lake road in the low December sunshine, with their sunlit peaks and buttresses separated by gulphs of blackness, have a kind of goblin brilliance that sets them apart from those almost featureless shapes upon whose hollows and crags alike the summer sun pours down. In March at Grasmere the new grass may be already a vivid green where the great meadow of the Boothwaite lies sheltered beneath the southern face of Helm Crag, while along the slopes towards Red Bank the shadowed western shores of the lake still sink, in all the sober colourings of the end of winter, into waters blurred with the vague mists of the last night's frost.

So before Mardale was drowned the cold, clear gloom of winter lingered in the hill-shadowed basin about the Dun Bull Inn, while along the sunnier shores of Haweswater the gorse was already in flower, and so the sunless hollow of Scales Tarn may be full of frozen shadows when the first bracken is beginning to uncurl on the great southward-facing slopes of the buttresses of Blencathra.

In our islands summer comes from the south, winter from the north. But here in Lakeland the seasons not only advance
170

and retreat along their accustomed level ways, so that spring is later on the Solway than about Morecambe Bay, and winter spreads south from the Border, but they climb and descend the fells, leisurely and fitfully, so that week by week summer may be watched rising with the fresh green of sprouting bracken up the slopes of Seat Sandal, or Maidenmoor, or Coniston Old Man, till they are green almost to the frost-shattered tops. And winter here sinks down upon the dales from above : indeed, it never really leaves the higher summits, Scafell and Skiddaw, Great Gable and Helvellyn, and their peers rise into altitudes from which winter only certainly retreats for the few hours of a sunny summer day.

With the fall of darkness, even in July and August, winter may often close about them again, and while tourists are peacefully sleeping beneath one blanket in the Rosthwaite hotels below, Scafell and the Gable endure amid the stars those remote rigours of frost and snow-squall which make the summer night a link between the arctic weather of one winter and the next. So in autumn winter hovers, visible, incarnate, above the dales ; now whitening one summit, now another ; creeping one morning so low that Helm Crag and Latrigg in their snows become one with the lonely whiteness of their greater brethren ; then shrinking upwards again until only a long streak of white on Fairfield's western slope and a patch or two on the dark fells above Easedale Tarn remind Grasmere of the coming winter ; so winter seems to step delicately about the dales before it finally descends into them.

THE LAKE COUNTRY (1930)

OVER this country, when the giant Eagle flings the shadow of his wing, the land is darkened. So compact is it that the wing covers all its extent in one pause of the flight. The sea breaks on the pale line of the shore ; to the Eagle's proud glance waves run in to the foot of the hills that are like rocks planted in green water.

From Whinlatter to Black Combe the clouds are never still. The Tarns like black unwinking eyes watch their chase, and the colours are laid out in patterns on the rocks and are continually changed. The Eagle can see the shadows rise from their knees at the base of Scawfell and Gable, he can see the black precipitous flanks of the Screes washed with rain and the dark purple hummocks of Borrowdale crags flash suddenly with gold.

So small is the extent of this country that the sweep of the Eagle's wing caresses all of it, but there is no ground in the world more mysterious, no land at once so bare in its nakedness and so rich in its luxury, so warm with sun and so cold in pitiless rain, so gentle and pastoral, so wild and lonely ; with sea and lake and river there is always the sound of running water, and its strong people have their feet in the soil and are independent of all men.

During the flight of the Eagle two hundred years are but as a day—and the life of man, as against all odds he pushes toward immortality, is eternal. . . .

CONISTON WATER

THE HIGH LEVEL ROUTE (1933)

YOU are now on the famous High Level Route to the Pillar *rock*, the rock-climbers' high road, clear in any mist by reason of the nail scratches and, besides that, marked every half-mile or so by tall cairns, which show clearly in front of you as the path winds round the projecting spurs. These spurs run down from Pillar Fell (the summit of which is now rising up above you on your left), into the dale bottom : but your own path, which is wonderfully contoured, keeps as good as a dead level, when it is once started on its way, and runs along the side of the mountain till it reaches its objective, the N.E. foot of the great mass of cliff known as the Pillar Rock. The foot of Pillar Rock is, like Looking Stead, on or near the 2000 contour : where the Rock joins the main fell on its top or S. side, that is at its back as you look up from the valley bottom, it is on the 2500 contour : the summit of Pillar Fell itself, a smooth top all grass grown, is a trifle under 3000. As you go along the High Level Route, all the way you have austere, magnificent prospects, changing in detail but not in quality, down Ennerdale and across it.

Perhaps this is the grandest half-hour's walk in the Lake District : and indeed in all " high level " routes, out along the horizontal fell-sides, where the gradients up and down are unbroken and seen in a *coup d'oeil*, there is a peculiar note of sombre and grandiose beauty. Here, certainly, with a touch of mist, the place is an El Greco picture, full of long distances and of wistful distortions, or round every bend you can expect to hear the wind moan through those rock-cut statues which guarded the entrance-way to Erewhon. You may walk in majesty along a high ridge-summit, and see the kingdoms of the earth spread at your feet ; or you may stand below some face of cliff, Lliwydd, Cheddar or Scafell Buttress, and look upwards humbly ; but to walk out horizontally into space and round projecting bastions, to have the feet sure enough to

173

free the eye, and to look both up and down in a kind of stolen grandeur, rapt half-way between earth and heaven, and confined by neither, is a peculiar happiness.

Sheep, the world's first surveyors, those most impassioned lovers of the rigid, undeviating contour, those steady, delicate, inflexible path-makers, first laid out these horizontal tracks, and they make them still on all the fells ; shepherds here and there have taken one of these tracks for their own use, and trodden the path wider and set a few stones on it ; then came the climbing age, and all the artifice of rope and nails and grandeur ; and Smith and Jones and Robinson have turned a shepherd's secret to a public benefit—Glyn Jones, John Robinson of the cairn, and Haskett Smith and many another good name and boot. All honour be to their memories ; for it is but the drums and tramplings of three brief generations of climbing men, conquering about the Pillar Rock, that have made this great and glorious highway. Let us then tread where they trod and continue the good work which they began ; for scree and falling water allow no prescriptive rights to the work of man's feet : therefore let us beat the bounds again and mark out our precarious claims by the impact of good nail and leather.

FEBRUARY SNOW (1938)

ONE winter afternoon I walked up the same valley on ski after a heavy fall of snow.

It was a day, rare in England, of clear sparkling brilliance and intense stillness, broken only by the distant conversation of some farmers trying the drifts for sheep around the lower " intakes " on the Grasmere side, and moving very slowly in the soft deep snow. The February sun was just warm enough to melt the surface of the snow in Tongue Ghyll, and it was possible to climb on ski without skis at an angle of about thirty degrees. The waterfall half-way up the valley had become a richly intricate design in glistening ice, some opaque, some translucent, smooth or mottled, here grass-centred spikes and columns against black moss, there glistening bulbs peeping out from the blankets of snow. Under Seat Sandal the snow had avalanched into thousands of snowballs of different sizes. The smooth ice on Grisedale Tarn reflected Dollywaggon Pike in pale gold with whorls of blown snow dull blue across it.

I took off my ski to explore the heaped-up drift by the wall that runs up Dollywaggon Pike, and reversed one of the ski-sticks, prodding deep into the snow all the way up. At the end of one prod, the stick fell loosely as the nob reached the air space round a sheep. In a few moments, with the aid of a coal shovel that I had in my rucksack, a rather disgruntled sheep was excavated. After it had tried to jump back into its comparatively warm cave, it was headed off and left to saunter down towards Thirlmere. The farmers say that if sheep are driven immediately on being dug out they are liable to collapse.

The sun had just left us and an icy sheen appeared on the snow. Below the saddle the first hollow looked surrealistically like a white cup sprinkled with a few tea leaves and in a few exhilarating moments, the darkness seeming to rush towards me, I was on the road sniffing the wood smoke of Grasmere.

175

SUNRISE ON SCAFELL (1938)

WHILE we curled up in our sleeping-bags under Mickledore, a faint afterglow was still warming the eastern hills and soon it was as dark as a clear night in June can ever be. The stillness at night on the hills is an experience. Above us hung the black wet crag of East Buttress, the steepest and most formidable crag in Lakeland. It overhangs considerably along almost the whole of its length, and, until a few years ago, was considered out of the question as far as climbing was concerned. The lead of Mickledore Grooves, without previous exploration, by Kirkus, started a wave of climbing on this crag, and the severity of most of these, for which Linnell and A. T. Hargreaves were responsible, was such that it raised the standard of possibility considerably for the whole of the sport.

The temperature even at 3,000 feet in midsummer can be almost at freezing point in the early hours, and our teeth were chattering as we set off about four o'clock for the Pulpit Rock, on Pikes Crag, facing Scafell Crag.

Slowly at first the sun touched the top of the West Wall, the Pinnacle and Pisgah, till they looked like towers and battlements of gold perched on the edge of a great blue-grey cliff against the palest of pale blue skies. As it picked out buttress after buttress it seemed to gather speed and soon the whole crag was ablaze. Down to the left the roof-like ridge of Mickledore sent its shadow down the line of Lord's Rake and parallel with Rake's Progress, the ledge above it from which the steep face of crag rises. Sharp thin shadows were cast by the cleavage along which run the Keswick Brothers' climb and Botterils Slab. Lighting up Central Buttress from the side, it picked out all the features of this great—some say greatest —rock climb.

The first ascent of Central Buttress, involving nearly 500 feet of continuous severity and exposure, was made by Herford,

176

Sansom and Holland in the spring of 1914, a wonderful climax to a great period of exploration on Scafell.

The Buttress sent its shadow over Moss Gill, the shadow from Pisgah was cast across Steep Gill upon the Pinnacle, whose Low and High Man cast theirs in turn upon the West Wall.

Mighty things have been achieved upon these bastions, and many a man grows old with a picture in his mind, that he conjures up sometimes by the fireside, of summer evenings on the Pinnacle. Everyone has gone home for dinner, the crag that has been in shadow all day wakes up and comes to fresh life as the sun sets ablaze all the significant detail of the sound grey rock face that stretches in a clean sweep upwards and downwards from his hands and feet.

SOURCES AND NOTES

1. From Camden's *Britannia*, originally published in Latin, 1586. The quotation is from the English translation edited by Edmund Gibson, 1695. Gibson was born at Bampton, Westmorland, and was Bishop of London from 1723 until his death in 1748.

2. From the " Preamble " to a poem called *The Fatall Nuptiall*, 1636, probably by Richard Brathwaite. See *Transactions* of the Cumberland and Westmorland Antiquarian and Archaeological Society, 1913.

3. From *The Journal of George Fox*, edited by Norman Penney, 1924, published in " Everyman's Library ". George Fox was the Founder of the Society of Friends.

4. From *The Journeys of Celia Fiennes*, edited by Christopher Morris, 1947, published by the Cresset Press.

5. From *An Essay towards a Natural History of Westmorland and Cumberland* by the Rev. T. Robinson, 1709. Robinson was Rector of Ousby, Cumberland, 1672–1719.

6. From *Tour through the Whole Island of Great Britain* by A Gentleman (i.e. Daniel Defoe) originally published in three volumes, 1724, 1725 and 1726. The *Tour through England and Wales* has been republished in " Everyman's Library ".

7. From *Description of the Lake at Keswick* by A Popular Writer, *i.e.* the Rev. John Brown, D.D., sometime Minor Canon of Carlisle Cathedral ; first published 1767, the year after Dr Brown's death, and often reprinted as being the earliest description of the district by a tourist.

8. From *A Six Months' Tour Through the North of England*, by Arthur Young. Young's enthusiasm for the scenery is the more surprising because he was primarily an agriculturist.

9. From *A Tour in Scotland 1769* by Thomas Pennant, the antiquary ; first published 1771, fourth edition 1776.

10 and 11. From the *Journal in the Lakes*, written by Thomas Gray, the poet, to his friend Dr. Wharton who should have accompanied him on his tour of the Lakes but was prevented by an attack of asthma. The extracts are taken from the version published in *The Works of Thomas Gray*, edited by Edmund Gosse, 4 volumes, 1884.

12. From *Observations on the Mountains, and Lakes of Cumberland, and Westmoreland* by the Rev. William Gilpin, 1786. Gilpin was a native of Cumberland and a lover of the picturesque.

178

13, 14 and 15. From *A Guide to the Lakes* by The Author of The Antiquities of Furness, 1778. The author was the Rev. Thomas West, a Roman Catholic priest, who died at Sizergh in 1779. This was the first guide-book to the Lakes and went through many posthumous editions, the eleventh being published in 1821.

16 and 17. From *A Survey of the Lakes* by James Clarke, land-surveyor, of Penrith. This large and entertaining work, with plans of the Lakes, was published in 1787 and a second edition in 1789.

18. From *A Fortnight's Ramble to the Lakes* by A Rambler, 1792. The author was Joseph Budworth, F.S.A., who later changed his name to Palmer. Two further editions of the book appeared, in 1795 and 1810.

19. Mrs. Radcliffe, the author of various " romances ", seems to have been the first woman tourist to venture up the mountains. The extract is part of her account of Skiddaw, printed in the later editions of West's *Guide*.

20. From William Wordsworth's letter to Dorothy Wordsworth, November 7, 1799 ; published in *The Early Letters of William and Dorothy Wordsworth*, edited by E. de Selincourt, 1935. Words-worth was born at Cockermouth 1770, went to school at Hawks-head, lived at Grasmere 1799–1813, and at Rydal 1813–50.

21. From S. T. Coleridge's letter to Thomas Poole, August 14, 1800 ; published in *Letters of Samuel Taylor Coleridge*, edited by E. H. Coleridge, 2 volumes, 1895. Coleridge lived at Greta Hall, Keswick, off and on for about six years from 1800.

22. From Charles Lamb's letter to William Wordsworth, January 30, 1801 ; published in *The Letters of Charles Lamb*, edited by Alfred Ainger, 2 volumes, 1891. In the end Lamb and his sister came to the Lakes in 1802 and stayed with the Wordsworths.

23 and 24. From The Grasmere Journal of Dorothy Words-worth, published in *Journals of Dorothy Wordsworth*, edited by E. de Selincourt, 1941, reprinted 1952.

25. From S. T. Coleridge's letter to Robert Southey, August 9, 1802 ; published as above (extract 19).

26, 27 and 28. From Wordsworth's Guide to the Lakes, origin-ally written as a long anonymous introduction to *Select Views in Cumberland, Westmoreland, and Lancashire* by the Rev. Joseph Wilkinson, 1810. The essay was published again with Words-worth's Duddon Sonnets, 1820, and as a separate " guide " in 1822, 1823 and 1835. The 1835 version, edited by E. de Selincourt, was reprinted by the Oxford Press in 1906.

29. From John Keats's letter to Thomas Keats, June 29, 1818 ; published in *The Complete Works of John Keats*, edited by H. Buxton Forman, 5 volumes, 1901, reprinted 1923.

30. From *A Guide to the Lakes* by William Green, 2 volumes, 1819. The author was an artist who lived at Ambleside and published many delightful drawings of the district.

31. From the Memoir printed amongst the Notes to Wordsworth's *The River Duddon : a Series of Sonnets, 1820*.

32. From *Confessions of an English Opium-Eater* by Thomas de Quincey, 1821. He lived at Dove Cottage, Grasmere, from 1809 until about 1830.

33. From *Guide to the Lakes* by Jonathan Otley, 1823. Otley was a native of Loughrigg and became a watch-maker at Keswick and a lifelong student of geology and natural history.

34. From *Tours to the British Mountains* by Thomas Wilkinson, 1824. He was a Quaker and lived at Yanwath and was a friend of the Wordsworths.

35 and 36. From *Colloquies* by Robert Southey, 1829. Southey lived at Greta Hall, Keswick, from 1803 until his death in 1843. He was Poet Laureate 1813–43.

37. From Hartley Coleridge's letter to Derwent Coleridge, August 30, 1830 ; published in *Letters of Hartley Coleridge*, edited by G. E. Griggs and E. L. Griggs and published by the Oxford Press in 1937. Hartley Coleridge lived at Ambleside 1823–30, Grasmere 1830–8 and Rydal 1838–49.

38. From *Sartor Resartus* by Thomas Carlyle, 1833.

39. From *Memoirs of the Life of Sir Walter Scott, Bart.* by J. G. Lockhart, 1837.

40. From *The Poetry of Architecture* by John Ruskin, 1838. This was written when Ruskin was barely twenty. He made his home at Brantwood, Coniston, in 1875 and died there in 1900.

41. From Hartley Coleridge's letter to Sara Coleridge, February 23, 1839 ; published as above (extract 35).

42, 43, 44 and 45. From de Quincey's *Reminiscences of the English Lake Poets* of which there are many editions. These extracts are taken from essays which originally appeared in Tait's *Edinburgh Magazine* and were revised and republished in de Quincey's collected Works, 1853, and *The Collected Writings of Thomas de Quincey*, edited by David Masson, 14 volumes, 1896.

46. From Dr. Arnold's letter to the Rev. J. Hearn, January 5, 1840 ; published in *The Life and Correspondence of Thomas Arnold, D.D.* by A. P. Stanley, 1844, 6th edition 1846. Dr. Arnold built

Fox How near Ambleside in 1833 and spent his holidays there until his death in 1841.

47 and 48. From *Recreations of Christopher North* by John Wilson, 1842. The extracts are from an essay " A Day at Windermere " originally published in *Blackwood's Magazine*. Wilson bought Elleray, Windermere, in 1807 and lived there until 1815 when he moved to Edinburgh and later became Professor of Moral Philosophy. He still owned Elleray, and came there for holidays, down to 1848.

49. From *Guide to the Lakes* by Harriet Martineau, 1855, 5th edition, 1876. Miss Martineau lived at The Knoll, Ambleside, 1846–76.

50. From *The Lazy Tour of Two Idle Apprentices* by Charles Dickens, published in *Household Words*, 1857.

51. From *Rambles in the Lake Country* by Edwin Waugh, 1861.

52. From *The Lake Country* by E. Lynn Linton, 1864. The author was the daughter of a former Vicar of Crosthwaite and the wife of W. J. Linton, wood engraver, of Brantwood, Coniston.

53. From *Essays of Travel* by R. L. Stevenson, written 1871, published 1876.

54. From Ruskin's preface to *A Protest against the Extension of Railways in the Lake District* by Robert Somervell, 1876.

55. From *Climbing in the British Isles* by W. P. Haskett Smith, 1894.

56, 57 and 58. From *The Lake Counties* by W. G. Collingwood, 1902. A new edition was published in 1932 (Warne) and another in 1938 (Dent). Mr. Collingwood, who was both an artist and an antiquary, lived and died at Coniston.

59. From *The English Lakes* by A. Heaton Cooper and W. T. Palmer, 1905. This book, of which several editions have appeared, was written by Mr. Palmer and illustrated by the late Mr. A. Heaton Cooper.

60. From *Months at the Lakes* by the Rev. H. D. Rawnsley, 1906. Canon Rawnsley was Vicar of Low Wray 1878–83, Vicar of Crosthwaite, Keswick, 1883–1917, and died at Grasmere in 1920. He was the author of *Literary Associations of the English Lakes*, 1894, and many books of essays and poems.

61. From *Chapters at the English Lakes* by the Rev. H. D. Rawnsley, 1913.

62. From *The Fairy Caravan* by Beatrix Potter (Mrs Heelis), 1929. A new edition was published in 1952. Miss Potter, afterwards Mrs. Heelis, who was the author and illustrator of *The*

Tale of Peter Rabbit and many other children's books, bought Hill Top Farm, Sawrey, in 1905 and lived at Sawrey until her death in 1943.

63. From *Must England's Beauty Perish?* by G. M. Trevelyan, 1929. This tract was published for the National Trust by Faber & Faber.

64 and 65. From *Days in Lakeland* by E. M. Ward, 1929, revised edition, 1948.

66. From *Rogue Herries* by Hugh Walpole, 1930. Sir Hugh Walpole lived at Brackenburn, Keswick, from 1924 until his death in 1941.

67. From *Walking in the Lake District* by the Rev. H. H. Symonds, 1933. This book has been reprinted several times.

68 and 69. From *The Hills of Lakeland* by W. Heaton Cooper, 1938.

INDEX TO AUTHORS

ARNOLD, Thomas (1795–1842): 125
BRATHWAITE, Richard (1588?–1673): 15
BROWN, John (1715–66): 25
BUDWORTH, Joseph (1756–1815): 52
CAMDEN, William (1551–1623): 13
CARLYLE, Thomas (1795–1881): 105
CLARKE, James (1744–92): 48, 51
COLERIDGE, Hartley (1796–1849): 104, 114
COLERIDGE, Samuel Taylor (1772–1834): 61, 69
COLLINGWOOD, W. G. (1854–1932): 151, 152, 153
DEFOE, Daniel (1660–1731): 23
DE QUINCEY, Thomas (1785–1859): 89, 115, 117, 120, 122
DICKENS, Charles (1812–70): 135
FIENNES, Celia (1662–1741): 18
FOX, George (1624–91): 17
GILPIN, William (1724–1804): 40
GRAY, Thomas (1716–71): 33, 37
GREEN, William (1760–1823): 83
HASKETT SMITH, W. P. (1861–1946): 149
HEATON COOPER, W. 175, 176
KEATS, John (1795–1821): 80
LAMB, Charles (1775–1834): 63
LINTON, E. Lynn (1822–98): 142
LOCKHART, J. G. (1794–1854): 107
MARTINEAU, Harriet (1802–76): 133
OTLEY, Jonathan (1766–1856): 93
PALMER, W. T.: 156
PENNANT, Thomas (1726–98): 30
POTTER, Beatrix (1866–1943): 163
RADCLIFFE, Ann (1764–1823): 55
RAWNSLEY, H. D. (1851–1920): 157, 160
ROBINSON, Thomas (?–1719): 21
RUSKIN, John (1819–1900): 109, 146
SOUTHEY, Robert (1774–1843): 97, 100

STEVENSON, Robert Louis (1850–94): 144
SYMONDS, H. H.: 173
TREVELYAN, G. M.: 165
WALPOLE, Hugh (1884–1941): 172
WARD, E. M.: 167, 170
WAUGH, Edwin (1817–90): 139
WEST, Thomas (1720–79): 42, 44, 46
WILKINSON, Thomas (1751–1836): 95
WILSON, John (1785–1854): 126, 129
WORDSWORTH, Dorothy (1771–1855): 65, 67
WORDSWORTH, William (1770–1850): 59, 70, 73, 76, 85
YOUNG, Arthur (1741–1820): 27

Printed in Great Britain by Butler & Tanner Ltd., Frome and London